CONTENTS

CRICKET'S BURNING PASSION

CRICKET'S BURNING PASSION

IVO BLIGH AND THE STORY OF THE ASHES

SCYLD BERRY AND RUPERT PEPLOE

Methuen

First published in Great Britain 2006 by
Methuen Publishing Ltd
11–12 Buckingham Gate
London
SW1E 6LB

10 9 8 7 6 5 4 3 2 1

A CIP catalogue record for this book is available from the British
Library.

ISBN-10: 0413776271
ISBN-13: 9780413776273

Typeset by SX Composing DTP, Rayleigh, Essex
Printed and bound in Great Britain by MPG Books, Bodmin, Cornwall

To our children:

Freya, Sceaf and Ankush   Julius and Arthur

LIST OF ILLUSTRATIONS

ACKNOWLEDGEMENTS

The publisher wishes to thank Medway Archives and Local Studies Centre. Extracts from the Bligh archive reproduced by kind permission of the Earl of Darnley and the Director of Community Services, Medway Council.

The publisher wishes to thank The Roger Mann Collection for permission to reproduce photographs. Other photos are from private collections.

FOREWORD

BY MICHAEL ATHERTON

In the aftermath of the wondrous 2005 Ashes series, a raft of cricket books appeared on the bookshelves. There was the usual gruesome mix of ghosted autobiographies, ghosted diaries and rushed, ill-considered reviews of what many thought to be one of the greatest Test series of all time. In all these accounts one thing was missing: why exactly did the smallest trophy in world sport inspire such feelings? For although the series itself was full to the brim with compelling cricket, and although the victory removed an increasingly weighty albatross from around English cricket's neck, there was seemingly something deeper, more meaningful, at stake. In other words, none of these accounts gave us any historical context at all. None of them told us exactly what the Ashes meant.

Thankfully, this book fills the gap, and here before us, lovingly told, is the story of the birth of the Ashes, what the authors describe as the Holy Grail of cricket. It is, at first glance, an unlikely story. Unlikely on many levels: the first England captain to bring back the Ashes from Australia wasn't an outstanding player; outwardly he didn't seem to be tough enough, suffering as he did from hypo-chondria; his team looked like a motley, disjointed bunch; and most of all it was hard to envisage this diffident, upper-class young man falling head over heels in love with a poor Australian girl from the outback, and then having the courage to withstand the objections of his family in order to marry her. Clearly, there was more to Ivo Bligh than met the eye.

From my perspective as a modern player it is both the differences and the similarities of Ivo's expedition that surprise. The differences are largely to do with the pace of the tour. The months-long boat trip allowed the captain plenty of time to ruminate in his private cabin and to set his thoughts down on paper; allowed his players time to acclimatise and get fit; and gave his party an adventure or two along the way. Indeed, an accident on the high seas almost meant that the Ashes never came into being. And then the tour itself, which allowed plentiful time for train journeys to country houses in order to enjoy the hospitality which, even then, seemed to be uniquely Australian. Little time left for practice and other irrelevancies.

Then there was the aftermath of Ivo's team's great triumph. The team weren't even sure if they had regained the Ashes or not, since a further game against an Australian team muddied the waters. Afterwards, most of the Ashes-winning cricketers of 1882/83 simply faded away into the background. Ivo himself pottered about his country pile impecuniously, forced to sell his family's collection of Old Master paintings to survive; others ran pubs, did a bit of coaching, died young or generally slipped away to little acclaim. Not for them a ticker-tape parade and a year exploiting, financially that is, the trappings of fame. At least this book has given them a little lasting immortality.

In one respect I found the similarities between the cricket of then and now absolutely striking. Victorian moralists had propagated the myth that cricket was the epitome of sport and that cricketers were the epitome of sportsmen. In 1921 Lord Harris was able to say of the phrase 'it's not cricket' that it represented the value system of a whole nation, that the phrase was 'in constant use on the platform, in the pulpit, in parliament and in the press, to dub something as being not fair, not honourable and not noble. What a tribute for a game to have won!'

A dozen years later, the manager of the MCC tour to Australia, Sir Pelham Warner, was quick to espouse these very British notions of fair play:

the very word 'cricket' has become synonymous for all that is true and honest. To say 'that is not cricket' is to imply something under-hand, something not in keeping with the best ideals . . . the aim of the MCC . . . in sending teams to all parts of the world is to spread the gospel of British fair play as developed in its national sport.

This, of course, was on the eve of the Bodyline tour which blew away such rose-tinted notions.

In this account, Scyld Berry and his co-author, a great-grandson of Bligh, show us that highly competitive cricket has always been the norm. In these low-scoring games (the ball dominated the bat much more than now) we see the same gripping tension as last summer; we see the players pushing the boundaries of what was considered to be fair as much as they do now. In 2005, the controversy surrounded England's use of substitutes. One hundred and twenty-two years before it concerned the running on the pitch with spiked boots by 'The Demon' Spofforth and Richard Barlow. Ashes cricket has rarely been played in a style which the Victorian moralists would have applauded. And for the honesty with which the authors deal with this we should be thankful.

Ivo Bligh, then, the unlikeliest of cricketing heroes, gave the game a legacy to cherish: a tiny terracotta urn which still inspires such feelings of desire. Much has changed since his time; much is still the same. As I write this, the latest England captain to regain the urn – Michael Vaughan – has just undergone a career-threatening operation. Ivo never played again for England after bringing home the Ashes; let us hope in that respect, at least, history does not repeat itself.

1
St Ivo's Quest

Joy, unadulterated but for a little alcohol, filled the Oval cricket ground on the late afternoon of 12 September 2005. Through the weeks of August the song had grown in volume and conviction: 'Coming home! Coming home! Ashes coming home!' and finally the lyric had come true. When England's captain Michael Vaughan lifted up a replica of a terracotta urn no more than four and a half inches high, and kissed it, the supporters of English cricket at the Oval and around the country were overjoyed.

Why was a thing so small the focus of such burning passion? Why did the tiniest of trophies mean so much to so many people, English and Australian, not to mention neutral observers of cricket around the world? The two teams had played superlative cricket for seven weeks, the stuff of Titans, in what was widely regarded as the most exciting Test series ever played. Rewards innumerable would come to the England players for winning: medals, bonuses, gifts, sponsorships, a meal-ticket for life in one or two cases. Yet the financial rewards flowed from this one glorious moment when no money was involved.

England had been ranked second in the World Test Championship organised by the International Cricket Council; Australia first. It was a fine achievement for number two, albeit with home advantage, to overcome number one, but their positions in the table remained the same. Clearly the joy was made greater by a wider historical context. It did not stem simply from the present feat of England defeating the strongest cricket country.

At the Oval six years earlier, in September 2000, England's cricketers and supporters had celebrated victory over West Indies. This was the first time England had won a series against them for 31 years. But the joy at beating Australia after a gap of 16 years, half the time-span, was infinitely greater. It transcended cricket followers, attracted – even gripped – those who had been indifferent to the sport, and affected the mood of the nation, as the open-top bus ride to Trafalgar Square the following day demonstrated. There was more to it than relief at England reversing a very long run of defeats.

An essential element was that England had beaten their oldest opponent, which West Indies were not. English emotion on this September day was fuelled by the knowledge that the contest for the Ashes had been going on for more than a hundred years; that the best cricketers in England had tried to defeat Australia, and had failed more often than not (up until 2006 Australia held the Ashes for 72 years, England for 50). The cricketers involved, and their supporters, felt the occasion was unique because the rivalry had gone on for so long so intensely. The cricket contest between England and Australia is the longest-standing continuous contest in any team sport. The annual cricket match between Canada and the United States of America began in 1844 but it has not been played continually ever since, or intensely.

Whatever the reasons for the significance of the Ashes, their symbolic power is captured on the urn itself, in the verse written anonymously, but presumably by a member of the staff of the Australian magazine, *Punch*. The poem was published in 1883, straight after England had won the Third Test against Australia in Sydney. All concerned reckoned at the time that England had therefore won the series by two matches to one. Hence the verse which celebrates the feat of the Honourable Ivo Bligh and his team:

> When Ivo goes back with the urn, the urn;
> Studds, Steel, Read and Tylecote return, return;
> The welkin will ring loud,
> The great crowd will feel proud,
> Seeing Barlow and Bates with the urn, the urn;
> And the rest coming home with the urn.

For the name of Barlow – Richard Barlow, an all-rounder from Lancashire – that of another Lancashire all-rounder, Andrew Flintoff, had to be substituted more than 120 years later. For the name of Bates – Billy Bates of Yorkshire, said by his captain Lord Hawke to have been the best batsman in England after Dr W.G. Grace – the name of Michael Vaughan had to be substituted. The second half of the verse can otherwise stand as well as any commemoration of that September day, when the great crowd felt proud

> Seeing Flintoff and Vaughan with the urn, the urn,
> And the rest coming home with the urn.

Cricket contests between England and Australia began with a match in Melbourne in March 1877. Historians have subsequently fixed on this as the first 'Test' match. The rivalry came alive and first demanded widespread public attention in August 1882, when Australia defeated England in England for the first time, at the Oval. The unprecedented defeat led to immediate calls for a captain and a team to go to Australia to avenge the defeat, thereby redeeming England's cricketing honour.

Six English cricket teams had toured Australia before 1882, though none with such a noble purpose. Those tours were organised entirely for commercial profit, either by the Australians – usually the Melbourne Cricket Club, counterpart of the Marylebone Cricket Club – or by the English entrepreneur James Lillywhite. A self-educated Sussex man, Lillywhite immersed himself in everything to do with cricket, from selling equipment and producing an annual to playing and promoting tours.

These six tours, however, had brought the growing sport as close to disrepute as popularity. The first two were wholesome enough, when the novelty was so great that the English team had to keep the whereabouts of a practice session secret in order to avoid the crowds: this was at the start of the inaugural tour of 1861/62. But the competitive element was not intense. The English XI on that tour and in 1863/64 had to play against local XXIIs, never eleven-a-side games, so low was the standard in Australia. In four consecutive games on the 1863/64 tour the Nottinghamshire bowler Robert Tinley took 98 wickets, with underarm lobs.

The next four English teams, starting in the 1870s, were broadly speaking either amateur or professional, but whichever they were, they did little credit to their country or their sport. A professional captain found it hard to enforce discipline, as a Sydney reporter of the 1876/77 tour observed: 'To play cricket successfully, it is necessary to have a clear head, a quick eye, and well-balanced nerves, qualities which I am compelled to admit were seldom exhibited by four or five of the All-England professional XI.'

The life of professional cricketers in the Victorian period was jolly, drunken and short. Often from poor backgrounds and without education, the professionals suddenly found themselves enjoying public esteem and earning relatively large sums: for a winter tour to Australia they would receive a fee of £200, sufficient to buy a better than average house. They knew, however, they were only going to earn such sums in their physical prime and were therefore going to *carpe diem* and live life to the full while they could. The insecurity of a professional sportsman's career was not followed by any security, financial or psychological, in retirement. Of the eleven professional players who toured Australia in 1881/82, ten were dead by 1908 – two of them suicides, another dying in a mental asylum. If Barlow, the Lancashire all-rounder, had a secret for his relative longevity (he lived to the age of 68), it was that he was an exception to the rule in being a teetotaller and non-smoker.

Cricketers from such a background were prone to gamble more than their own lives away. They gambled on the voyage out to Australia – on horse-races in England, on their own foot-races and other games aboard ship – and they gambled when they landed. The new settlements in Australia, gripped with gold-rush fever, were every bit as keen on betting as they were, starting with the simple tossing of a coin, or 'two-up'. It was asking too much of these cricketers, in the absence of the ICC's Anti-Corruption and Security Unit, to refrain from betting while on tour – even on matches in which they were playing. England had no specialist wicketkeeper for the first of all Tests in 1876/77 because Ted

Pooley had to remain in New Zealand awaiting trial. A bet on a game in Christchurch with a member of the public had turned nasty, a hotel room had been trashed by several English players, and Pooley, after being detained by police, was remanded on bail before being acquitted of assault. When players were not supplementing their tour fees by betting on the cricket, John Selby of Nottinghamshire was running sprint races, and allegedly allowing the local champion to win the first race before he won the second race at greater odds. A county colleague of Selby's, Alfred Shaw, wrote of the 1876/77 party under Lillywhite: 'Some of the members of our team, who need very small encouragement at any time to back their opinions and statements, were led to participate in enterprises they had better eschewed.'

No ethical improvement was discernible by the time of the 1881/82 tour of Australia. The English professionals backed themselves at 30-1 to win the match against Victoria when they were on the verge of losing. They won both the match and their money, while other rumours abounded. The most persistent was that two of them had tried to lose a game for a bet, and beat up a third player in the touring party who informed on them. Selby protested his innocence in a letter to MCC on his return to England, but he was to end up in a law court before he died, aged 44.

The first of the two English teams containing amateurs was no better behaved. Amateur cricketers, who charged only expenses, were normally public school and sometimes Oxbridge educated and were supposed to set a sporting example. In 1873/74 Dr W.G. Grace decided that a tour of Australia would make a nice free honeymoon for himself and his new wife Agnes, and he charged £1,500 for his services, plus lavish expenses, including all that he could drink, which was not inconsiderable. And while the captain and four other Gloucestershire amateurs travelled first-class, the professionals went second-class, stayed in inferior hotels, and were paid one-tenth of W.G.'s fee, £150, much less than for previous tours. The *Sydney Mail* referred to the 'gentlemen and professional players reversing their respective social positions', adding that James Southerton and James Lillywhite (without a Mr or Esq. between them) were 'the most gentlemanly and unassuming members of W.G. Grace's All-England XI.'

The English team of 1878/79 under Lord Harris consisted of amateurs, except for two professionals to do most of the bowling, and while they were better behaved, they were too weak to be considered anything like representative of English cricket. Even then they were embroiled in controversy and violence when spectators, angered by an umpiring decision, invaded the field at Sydney and Harris was hit on the back, possibly by a stick, as play was suspended. Betting was at the core, as in most cricket riots outside Asia, and the Sydney crowd was made more dissatisfied by the umpire being a Victorian.

To become attractive to all sections of society, to achieve integrity, to become the sport of empire, cricket needed to raise its game. A fresh leader was required to set an example and to close the traditional English social divide by unifying amateurs and professionals in a team which represented the strength of English cricket; a leader who would select players who did not bet on the matches they were playing in; a leader who promoted team spirit, in contrast to the amateur captains who had been autocratic and self-indulgent or the professional captains who had not imposed discipline; a leader who could give eloquent speeches in contrast to most of his inarticulate predecessors; a captain who could field well himself and who would promote good fielding as the manifestation of the moral health of his team; a captain who had a cricket brain and who could bring the best out of his players.

Cometh the hour, cometh the captain: a 23-year-old, who remains the youngest man to have led England in a Test match against Australia.

*　*　*

The nine-year-old new boy was unusually tall for his age, and unusually diffident for his class. In his early days at Cheam, an elite preparatory school which sent many of its boys to nearby Eton, it was not apparent whether he had the thick skin to survive the scrutiny of his peers and elders. The diffidence was a veneer easily punctured by the cruel barbs at which confident boys excelled.

Letters home by the nine-year-old new boy, the Honourable Ivo Bligh of Cobham Hall in Kent, still capture his unhappiness.

> The boys have been bullying me dreadfully today – they have been knocking me about all class time, nearly all of my class and I daren't tell the monitors lest they should call me a blab. I wish something could be done and then they get me into a scrape by saying to the Master it was all Bligh's fault. I am afraid I have nothing else to say. I remain your affectionate son, Ivo.

Like most of his letters home during his life, Ivo addressed it to his father, the Sixth Earl of Darnley – or in Ivo's eyes 'My dearest papa' – not to his father and mother jointly. His mother was not someone to be troubled at the best of times, let alone when emotions were involved. She was a daughter of the Earl of Chichester, a very tall lady renowned for being 'as stiff as a ramrod and as frigid as a glacier', according to the family history, *The Lords of Cobham Hall.* Her idea of a warm welcome was to extend a limp left hand and murmur 'How do you do', without expecting an answer.

Ivo's next letter home was only slightly more cheerful. 'I am quite well but very lonely – no-one of the boys will admit into their cricket matches and so I go about and look at them playing. Little Cust (this is Ivo's cousin) is the only boy I can talk to without being called Nellie Bligh.' Nellie Bligh was Cockney rhyming slang for 'fly'. It was also an old, now archaic name for someone of low birth and limited capabilities.

A week later, on 9 May 1868, the tone was still wretchedness: 'I hope you will come and see me again very soon as I am still dreadfully lonely – if you could come and see me very often for a little while I might get over it but as it is now I cannot give you a much better account of myself.' Hope was at hand, though, as the date suggests. The cricket season was moving into full swing and although Ivo had at first not been allowed to play in the boys' matches, his abilities were apparent as soon as he was given a chance.

On 17 May he reported home: 'I am considered a swell bowler

and am most likely going to be out in the third ground which of course is a higher ground than the fourth where I am at present.' The next day, on 18 May, happiness can be detected for the first time; the new boy is going to swim not sink.

> I think I have told you that I have been put up into a higher cricket ground than I was before. I was in the lowest one before but now I am in the higher one where most of the older boys play. I am second in my class now – the mathematical examination is very difficult and I can answer few of the questions which we put on the slate – they are all about troy and ounce weights about which I do not know an atom. I am getting on well. I remain your affectionate son, Ivo.'

As his father was at various times President of MCC and President of Kent County Cricket Club, and the Darnley family had for several generations been the most prominent cricketing family in the county of Kent if not the whole country – the Fourth Earl of Darnley captained Kent against Hampshire at Lord's in the eighteenth century – the son knew his father would be especially pleased by his progress in the family tradition. Above all, cricket and its friendships offered Ivo a warm and friendly surrogate for the mothering he seems to have been partially denied.

For being able to make an immediate impact on the cricket fields of Cheam School, and thereby to earn himself a popularity which saved him from bullying and relentless teasing, Bligh had to thank one of the leading professional cricketers of the day, George Bennett. 'Farmer' Bennett, as he was known, worked as a bricklayer at the Bligh family home of Cobham Hall, and from 1864 to 1874 was the cricket professional at Eton, doubtless on the Earl of Darnley's recommendation. Bennett knew the trick of tossing the ball up at Cobham, where the pitch was aligned east to west, so that it came out of the evening sun; and although he never did correct Ivo's bottom-handed grip which prevented his bat coming down vertically in defence, on hearing of Bennett's death Bligh called him 'a wonderfully good coach for young cricketers'.

Before Eton, Bennett went on a great adventure to the other side of the earth. In the first cricket tour ever made to Australia, by an English or any other team, Bennett was selected as the sole representative of Kent. The majority of the twelve cricketers came from Surrey, starting with the captain Heathfield Stephenson. A photograph taken shortly before they set out on their voyage in October 1861 suggests a tough, knowing band of fellows, ready to take a risk in search of self-improvement or at least a winter's wage. Once they arrived in Australia after two whole months at sea, they played their first game in Melbourne after practising 'in camera'. The second, after a 200-mile coach journey on a rough road into the interior of Victoria, was at Beechworth. Bennett's round-arm bowling had been good enough to polish off XVIII of Victoria by an innings in the opening match, and in the game against a local XXII in Beechworth he took eleven wickets for 10 runs in the first innings. (In 1828 MCC allowed the bowler to raise his hand as high as his elbow; in 1864 overarm bowling, above shoulder height, was authorised.) To this day not many English bowlers in Australia have recorded better figures than Bennett at Beechworth.

From Cheam school, which now claims the Duke of Edinburgh and Prince Charles among alumni, Ivo went on to Eton. He had originally wanted to avoid the rough-and-tumble of another new school, and asked his father to let him be privately educated by a tutor at home, before going into the Royal Engineers: he had conceived a romantic notion of joining the Engineers after seeing them at Chatham. His father sent him to Eton, however, to be tutored by Mr Joynes, who had taught at Cobham Hall in the 1840s. The Earl of Darnley knew that Joynes would keep an eye on his boy, in return for occasional presents of venison from the Darnley estate. With a sometimes tangible obsequiousness Joynes reported that 'Ivo always seems remarkably attentive' and 'very pleasant and docile', although 'sometimes late with his verses'. Joynes even warned the Earl that his son 'should take care his popularity is not a snare to him'. When Ivo decided that he was not constitutionally suited to the Engineers, or Army training at Sandhurst, he swotted up on his Latin verses to get into Trinity College, Cambridge. His best friends, Edward and Alfred Lyttelton, with whom he played Eton Fives and racquets, were bound for Trinity; and at university, unlike Sandhurst, Ivo would have the opportunity to play the sports at which he was becoming almost effortlessly accomplished.

Having gone up to Trinity in the autumn of 1877, Ivo was soon awarded his Blue for racquets, tennis and cricket. He had already played an important innings, not for Eton, but for Eighteen of North Kent against the United South XI: at the age of sixteen he had scored 35 against some of the best bowlers in England, including W.G. Grace himself. At lawn tennis he was unbeaten in 1879 and 1880, whether in singles or in doubles with his partner Alfred Lyttelton. His height of 6ft 3in, his long reach and his whippy wrists served him well in batting too. Ivo gained his Blue in his first season of 1878, when the University won every first-class match. He was a fine fielder too, firstly in the outfield (at Eton one sports day he had thrown the cricket ball 96 yards), and often as long stop before the standard of wicketkeeping improved and the position became obsolete; he then moved to point. In 1880, when he scored over a thousand runs at an average of 30 for Cambridge and Kent, he had the second-highest first-class aggregate in the country. For the University against Yorkshire, so often the strongest of the counties in bowling, Bligh scored 70 and 57 not out by means of 'brilliant batting'. He became a regular for the main fixture of the domestic season, Gentlemen v Players, and came close to selection for England v Australia in the Oval Test: it was between him and W.G. Grace's younger brother Fred for the last batting place. Fred played, made a 'pair', and died from pneumonia within a fortnight.

While Ivo was embarking on what seem destined to be a brilliant career, a girl called Florence Morphy was growing up in Australia. She had been born in Beechworth, in August 1860, a year and a half before 'Farmer' Bennett and his fellow English cricketers had played there on the inaugural cricket tour of Australia. Her father had been a gold commissioner and police magistrate in Beechworth before his sudden death from apoplexy in July 1861. It was a tough job in the gold-fields, issuing mining licences, which had to be renewed every month, and keeping control over rootless men who lived in tents, often surrounded by mud, and drank, and vented their anti-Chinese feelings. Ned Kelly was marauding through these parts by the end of the 1870s.

Florence was the seventh and last of Morphy's children, and the most resourceful. From her Irish father she inherited reddish-auburn hair and thin lips; from her Kentish mother the social graces. A photograph of the young Florence shows a handsome, almost classical face, like that of a Greek goddess. The eyebrows suggest the strength of character. 'It became increasingly obvious that the "baby" of the family, Florence, was extremely intelligent and versatile; also her exceptional looks and natural charm began to turn heads and halt conversations.' So wrote Ronald Willis after researching Florence's early years for his book *Cricket's Biggest Mystery*. 'These attributes, allied with a sound education and grounding in the social graces, won her access to wealthy and influential circles.' The widow Morphy, on a government pension, moved her family to the Hawthorne suburb of Melbourne. By 1881, when the leading family (in wealth and social standing) in the colony of Victoria needed a governess/piano-teacher for their daughters, Miss Florence Morphy was such a suitable applicant that she secured the post. She moved to live with the Clarke family at their newly built mansion of Rupertswood, at Sunbury, near Melbourne.

* * *

There is more however to the tradition of the Ashes than winning and losing, however long the timescale. What Bligh did, unlike previous English cricket captains, was to set out on a quest which touched a chord in the national consciousness. Here, for the first time in cricket, was the oldest of human narratives: a story of life, then death, followed by a quest which ends successfully in regeneration.

For Australians, the Ashes have their own significance. To hold them is to prove their manhood, their own fitness as a nation. The overtones are social, cultural, psychological. The offspring of the Mother Country has proved stronger than the parent when Australia hold the Ashes. Australia defeating England at cricket was part of the process which ended in the colonies standing on their own independent feet as the Commonwealth of Australia in 1901.

For the English follower of cricket, there is another resonance, a deeper one, which it is no exaggeration to say is mystical, even religious. The Ashes have often been called cricket's 'Holy Grail'. The myth of the Holy Grail is confined to western Christendom, and specifically to the Anglo-French tradition, where it has become interwoven with Celtic myths. One common version has it that Joseph of Arimathea brought the chalice which Jesus Christ used for the Last Supper from Jerusalem to Avalon, somewhere not far from Glastonbury. Since then, knights beginning with Sir Lancelot and Sir Galahad have dedicated their chivalrous lives to the quest for the Holy Grail, hidden and elusive.

When Bligh set forth to Australia, in a less secular age than today, he was frequently called 'St Ivo', especially in verse in popular periodicals, English and Australian. Partly this must have been because he was surely the saintliest man to captain England at cricket, before or since. But also, from the outset, the English attempt to regain the Ashes had these religious overtones, both of a quest to regain the equivalent of the Holy Grail, and of a crusade. The body of English cricket had been killed and seized from its rightful sepulchre, and now St Ivo was leading the attempt to recover the ashes at the first opportunity. He was another knight on another romantic quest. The parallels even extended to the object of the quest being a cup or 'graal' in medieval English, a vessel of little worldly value yet beyond all price. The difference between the grail and the urn lay merely in the contents.

A football match between England and Germany, or two Latin American countries, will have an historical context. A heavyweight championship boxing final between a black man and a white man, between Joe Louis of the USA and Max Schmeling of Nazi Germany, will have implications beyond the field of sport. But nothing in team sport extends so far back into the past, or perhaps so deeply into the subconscious, as the contest for cricket's Ashes.

Bligh's quest was romantic in a second sense. Born of a mother who was famed for her iciness, brought up in the all-male worlds of Eton and Cambridge, he was ready for a relationship with an

Australian woman two years younger than he; and without this romance, we shall see, the idea of the Ashes would not have been turned into substance, or at least not as soon as it was. This idea was conceived at the Oval in 1882, but had still to take a physical form. Bligh's relationship with the Clarke family, and his romance with Florence Morphy, brought into existence the famous and fragile urn, of which Vaughan held aloft a replica on that September day, and kissed it for all the world to see. His quest had succeeded. A quest which will go on so long as human beings seek escape from reality in sport.

2

The Concept

Test cricket came of age on 29 August 1882. It had been born five years earlier in March 1877 when the first international match between Australia and England had been played in Melbourne. But the first eight of these international matches, as they were called, had not produced anything to excite the public imagination; and the same could be said of the international matches between Canada and the United States of America, which had started in 1844. A catalyst was required to ignite public interest – a contest that would demonstrate the dramatic possibilities of international cricket. The defining moment came on 29 August 1882, on the second day of the Oval Test match, the only one of this summer.

The moment when Test cricket came of age can even be fixed as the afternoon of that second day at Kennington Oval. The exact time can almost be determined too, at around five o'clock in the afternoon. It was a cold, autumnal day which had started wet, and the shivering crowd of 20,000 must have sensed they were witnesses to a new phenomenon – the mass commercialisation of international sport, so it turned out – as they sat in the wooden stands or the pavilion, or craned for a view in the spaces in between, while England's score, and time, appeared to stand still.

The play on the first day of this Test had not differed from the eight previous matches. The pitch had been poor, bowlers had dominated, and the contest had not been dramatically close (the closest victory margins so far had been 45 runs and four wickets). Australia had batted first and been dismissed for 63, the lowest total of their entire tour. It cannot have been a '63 all-out pitch' because Billy Murdoch had won the toss and chosen to bat first, and when his champion bowler Frederick Spofforth looked back at Australia's innings in his old age he said: 'I might speak for myself, and say I was disgusted, and thought we should have made at least 250.'

Spofforth accused his batsmen of 'lack of nerve' on the big occasion. Yet in their defence it can be advanced that the Australian team had been playing in England since 15 May, had only thirteen men to call on for their 38-match tour, and were depleted by injury. 'I am very sorry to say that the incessant toil has interfered sadly with the physique of our men' wrote an unidentified member of this Australian team in the *Sydney Mail.* 'I wish heartily that this great match had taken place about two months ago instead of now, when the men are all knocked up.' Australia's eleven players picked themselves as the off-spinner George Palmer had a groin strain, and Percy McDonnell was also injured, so that Alexander Bannerman had to play with a split finger.

England however did not bat substantially better and were dismissed for 101 by the close of the opening day. Spofforth destroyed them, bowling throughout to take seven wickets for 46. He had not been at his best for most of the tour, neither so fast nor as effective as he had been on the tours of 1878 and 1880. In the former summer Spofforth had been hailed as the bowler of the age, after he had run through the strong MCC side twice in a day at Lord's, taking ten wickets for only 20 runs, and had set up the most surprising victory which cricket had seen to this point; for Englishmen had never expected that Australians could play cricket so well as they, let alone better. In 1882 Spofforth had played every match for the first two months then broken down with a thigh strain: although he was 6ft 3in tall, he weighed less than ten and a half stone and had no spare meat on him. Forced to rest and recover, Spofforth returned to the Australian side a fortnight before the Oval Test and to the form which had given him the sobriquet of 'The Demon'.

The second day, a Tuesday, dawned with rain, but play had to go on because of the commercial imperatives. The Australian players, bar Bannerman, had each put up £100 (roughly equivalent to £6,000 today) as an advance to cover tour expenses; and on the tour they took 50 per cent of the takings at the turnstiles (nothing from the members). The resumption was postponed to allow some time for drying out, but only from 11.30 until 12.10, and then the ground was still wet. England's left-arm medium-pacer Richard Barlow, who featured in Francis Thompson's poem 'At Lord's', scraped mud out of the footholds with the studs which were to become controversial on Bligh's tour that winter, and had the groundsman fill them with sawdust. The ball was going to be awkward for the bowler to grip, awkward for the England fielders to stop. The advantage lay with the batsmen, who would find the ball skidding on, until the sun came out and the drying pitch cut up so the bounce became unpredictable.

If the Australian batting failed a second time – dismissed for 122 – it was not for want of nerve in one case at least. Their opener Hugh Massie was a hitter, as well as a banker by profession like Spofforth, and he seized this moment to hit 55 runs in 45 minutes. While his opening partner Bannerman blocked, Massie scored nine fours – mostly with lofted drives to leg – and some of them would have been six today (before 1910 the ball had to be struck out of the ground to count six). Massie knocked the arrears off the board and the bowlers off their length. He was dropped at long-off when 38 by Alfred Lucas, who was not going to be England's candidate for Man of the Match. Although the Australians then collapsed again, they had a target of 85 to defend on a pitch which was made for Spofforth even more than in England's first innings.

At 3.45 p.m. on 29 August England began their run-chase, in sprightly fashion. England's captain was not Dr W.G. Grace, even though he was playing and opening the batting, but Albert Hornby, captain of Lancashire, and the other half of Thompson's haunting refrain. Hornby was short of stature but not self-confidence or impetuosity (he was stumped twice in one of his three Tests). Having gone in at number ten in England's first innings, which it could be argued was his correct position in a powerful batting line-up, he decided to open the second innings instead of Barlow. Earlier that summer, Barlow had taken two and a half hours to score 5 not out against Nottinghamshire; an innings which had driven one of his opponents – William Barnes, now an England team-mate – to borrow a term from the American Civil War and call Barlow a Stonewaller. Hornby batted at the tempo which is recognised today as being the best for knocking off a small target, but did not have the technique to go beyond 9, which was to remain his highest Test score. Two balls later Barlow, who had been demoted to number three, was, like Hornby, bowled by Spofforth, although this time it was off an inside edge.

England had reached 15 for two wickets, but so long as Grace was batting, England were going to win. In the previous Test at the Oval, in 1880, England had been set an even more paltry target by Australia, and had collapsed to 31 for five in pursuit of 57, but Grace, who had scored 152 as an opener in the first innings and done a lot of bowling and wanted a rest, had come in at number seven to knock off the runs. Now the finest amateur cricketer in England was joined by the finest professional, George Ulyett of Yorkshire, who was the Ian Botham of his day. Not only a fast bowler, he could hit the ball a long way (one of his hits at Edgbaston was measured at 130 yards) and, like Botham, he once scored 149 against Australia. Together they took England's score up to 50 and Ralph Barker, the historian who recreated the 1882 Oval Test in 'Ten Great Bowlers', wrote that bookmakers on the ground were offering 60-1 against an Australian win.

One reason why Test cricket had not taken off before this match may have been the lack of duels within the team game: no Bradman v Larwood, no Hutton v Lindwall, no Flintoff v Warne. In the eight previous Tests the two champions of their day, Grace and Spofforth, had not played against each other. Grace had toured Australia before Test cricket, in 1873/74, when he had noted the 20-year-old Spofforth as a 'very fair bowler' with a strong throwing arm. When they had faced each other in the famous MCC match at Lord's in 1878, and Spofforth had hit Grace's stumps, knocking a bail back 30 yards, Spofforth in his excitement had shouted 'Bowled!' – which might have prompted a warning from an ICC Match Referee. They were alike in being intensely competitive, yet opposite: batsman v bowler, English v Australian, The Champion v The Demon. Grace and Spofforth were the first two cricketers to be acknowledged as having celebrity status in that they were the first two cricketers to be the subject of Spy cartoons in *Punch*, the 1870s equivalent of 'This Is Your Life'.

Spofforth, having started by bowling fast with his wicketkeeper standing back, switched from the gasworks end to the pavilion end to try and break England's third-wicket partnership: this switching of ends was to become one of his familiar, even notorious, schemes. Sir Neville Cardus, calling on impressionism, wrote of Spofforth that he was 'a stark man who let in with him the coldest blast of antagonism that ever blew over a Test field'. 'A Country Vicar' called on his religious background to write: 'he had rather the type of countenance which one associates with the Spirit of Evil in <u>Faust</u>. A long face, somewhat sardonic; piercing eyes; a hooked nose; and his hair, parted in the middle, giving the impression of horns.' Spofforth was the Bill O'Reilly, the Dennis Lillee, the Glenn McGrath of his day, a bowler who disliked all batsmen, judging by the disgust he felt at those on his own side in 1882. He would seem to have been the first bowler to give an incoming batsman the glare.

For his spell from the pavilion end Spofforth cut his run to nine yards, brought his keeper up and bowled mainly off-cutters. The calligraphic effect of his bowling was enhanced by a leap into the air before his delivery stride: 'a final bound at the wicket', Ivo Bligh called it. He was also recognised as the first modern bowler in that he bowled with a high arm, whereas English bowlers were still nearer to round-arm. Another unusual feature was Spofforth's follow-through: as he ran in at an angle, almost from mid-off, he followed through on to the line of the stumps and ran down the pitch. This was to become the *casus belli* on Bligh's tour that winter. And Spofforth followed through so vigorously that his right hand almost touched the ground.

Above all, Spofforth was a thinking bowler. Coming from Sydney, where baseball was the winter game, unlike in Melbourne, Spofforth was fascinated by the aerodynamics of a cricket ball. This was *terra incognita* as much as parts of Australia were, and in trying to work out the physical laws Spofforth consulted a university professor before advancing his theory that a cricket ball could move in one of four directions while in the air: to off, or to leg, or downwards (in other words over-spin), or upwards (back-spin). Like a baseball pitcher, he experimented with changes of pace ahead of bowlers in England, sometimes holding only one half of the ball in order to slow it down, or delivering his fast yorker, all without any change of action. Or he thought that nobody could detect the changes, and worked out a signalling system with his wicketkeeper Jack Blackham, but he reckoned without some clever clogs from Cambridge. Spofforth had actually refused to play in the inaugural Test in 1876/77 because the selectors had picked Blackham ahead of Murdoch. As Jack Pollard notes in *Australian Cricket*, Spofforth considered his partnership with state colleague Murdoch 'vital to his success'. By 1882 it was no longer an issue because Blackham concentrated on keeping and Murdoch on the captaincy. (As a captain Murdoch led Australia in sixteen Tests, winning five and losing seven.)

A photograph giving a general view of the Oval during the 1882 Test, in the MCC collection, shows no visible difference between the pitch being used for the match and the rest of the ground: it was all of the same colour and texture. On such a natural, damp and little-rolled pitch, off-cutters of medium pace are the most effective form of bowling, economical yet penetrative. Moreover, Victorian batsmen in the main used their bats, not their pads, to defend their stumps. Of Spofforth's 94 Test wickets, all taken against England, 49 were bowled.

At 51 for two Ulyett edged Spofforth and was caught behind. Lucas replaced Ulyett – and suddenly England had two new batsmen at the crease, for Grace was gone too, after winning his duel with Spofforth up to a point. Grace had been facing the metronomic accuracy of the right-arm medium-pacer Harry Boyle, a tough gold-miner from Bendigo, and had reached 32 in a hurry, to finish the game on this second evening before the turf was completely cut up. One of Spofforth's schemes had been to place a silly mid-on for

Grace, as nobody else had dared, to cramp him in his legside hits; and Murdoch posted a silly mid-on for Grace when Boyle too was bowling. When Grace went to drive Boyle, he aimed to the off not to leg, and was caught at mid-off by Bannerman, making England 53 for four wickets.

Grace's replacement was the Honourable Alfred Lyttelton, a friend of Bligh's and an all-rounder in every sense. He represented Cambridge University at real tennis, racquets – as a pair with Bligh – and athletics as well as cricket. He could not only bat but also keep wicket (an average of 27 was very high for a wicketkeeper-batsman of his time) and represented England at football too. He trained at the Bar, became a MP and Colonial Secretary in Balfour's government. Above all else, in these circumstances, Lyttelton knew the secret of Spofforth's action. For Lyttelton's brother was the Honourable Edward Lyttelton, who was the cricket captain of Cambridge in 1878 (before he played for England at football and became headmaster of Eton). In later life Bligh recalled how Edward Lyttelton had prepared the Cambridge team for their match against the 1878 Australians:

> Our captain, Edward Lyttelton, coached us in the peculiarities of Spofforth's bowling. He showed us that if we watched his hand carefully we should notice that when he was going to bowl his fast yorker his hand would be held straight out facing us, whereas when a break was coming the hand would be parallel to his chest. I think the coaching was of some use. At any rate, we won the match in an innings.

Armed with this knowledge Alfred Lyttelton began confidently, or at least more so than Lucas. He glanced Boyle for 2 then hit a boundary when he 'turned Spofforth neatly to long leg for four', according to Barker; it sounds as though Lyttelton had spotted the off-cutter. But had he told the secret to all his team-mates? Had there been any team-talk in the build-up to the Test? The eve of the game had been a Sunday and the England team, amateurs and professionals, might not have met until the morning of the match.

A few singles accrued and England's total reached 65 for four.

Only 20 runs to win, six wickets left. The Australians could have been forgiven for easing off: Spofforth had been bowling at one end or the other for the whole game as Murdoch used only three bowlers, Tom Garrett the other. The Australians did not ease off though. They had their pride, as all cricket teams representing Australia have had pride; for although there was no political entity known as Australia, these Victorians and New South Welshmen and the one South Australian, George Giffen, had a collective identity and felt loyalty to a greater whole. They had their own colours – red, black and yellow – as England did not.

The Australians had another motivation for not easing off and letting England win. They were still incensed by the incident earlier in the match when Grace, they thought, had been guilty of bad sportsmanship. Here is another reason why Test cricket can be said to have been born on this day. The intensity of the cricket was raised by this incident to the level which has prevailed in Ashes Tests ever afterwards, for nothing incites or excites a player like the accusation of cheating.

As Australia, after Massie's counter-attack, had collapsed in their second innings on the Tuesday morning to 122, Sammy Jones was run out by Grace for 6. Or rather Jones was given run out by the umpire Bob Thoms when it seems that he should not have been, for the ball was dead. The best account comes to us from the other umpire, Luke Greenwood, who had been a first-class cricketer himself, unlike Thoms. Greenwood was interviewed by 'Old Ebor', A.W. Pullin, in the valuable book *Talks With Old Yorkshire Cricketers*. In his 64th year Greenwood remembered: 'I umpired for the Australians on three visits. They always behaved like gentlemen to me, and I never saw teams work better together.' It was an early reference to the team spirit possible when there was no distinction between amateur and professional.

Greenwood went on to describe Grace's running out of Jones, who was the youngest member of the Australian team at 21.

In the Australians' second innings W.L. Murdoch and S.P. Jones were batting. Mr Murdoch hit the ball a little on the leg side, and the

Hon. A. Lyttelton, who was keeping wicket for England, ran for it and threw it in to Peate, who was at short slip. The run was made safely enough, and Peate made no attempt to take up the ball. Mr Jones thereupon walked out of his ground to pat the wicket where the ball had risen at the previous delivery, and W.G. Grace coolly picked up the ball, walked to the wicket, dislodged the bails, and cried, 'How's that?' Thoms, who was the umpire appealed to, gave him 'out', and out Mr Jones had to go. Mr Murdoch, on seeing what had occurred, remarked, 'That's very sharp practice, W.G.'; and to this day I think it was. Had I been appealed to I should not have given Jones out, for the ball was to all intents and purposes dead, and there had been no attempt to make a second run.

It was when 20 runs still remained for England to win, with six wickets left, that the score, and time, or so it felt, stood still. Spofforth, incensed by the wrong done by Grace to the youngest member of his team, had declared in the dressing-room, before England chased their target of 85: 'This thing can be done.' Boyle bowled a maiden at Lyttelton, Spofforth a maiden at Lucas. Boyle bowled a second consecutive maiden at Lyttelton, and Spofforth at Lucas, then a third maiden each; and a fourth. The over in Test cricket consisted of four balls in the 1880s (in the 1890s it was increased to five balls in England and six in Australia). Four-ball overs wasted about half-an-hour per day in more frequent changing of ends, compared to a six-ball over, so the number of balls bowled per hour was sometimes not much more than now. In England's second innings at the Oval, with wickets falling, Australia's rate was down to seventeen six-ball overs an hour.

Boyle bowled his fifth consecutive maiden at Lyttelton; so did Spofforth at Lucas. 'The crowd lapsed into a heavy silence' Barker wrote,

and the tinkling of hansom cabs along the Harleyford Road could be clearly heard. The remaining batsmen, watching through the closed windows of the committee room, shivered with a mixture of cold and fright. Every cricketer knows what it is like to wait for his knock in a tight corner when he cannot keep warm. A.G. Steel's teeth were chattering; he could not keep his jaw still. Barnes's teeth would have been chattering too if he had had any, but he wore false teeth and had taken them out . . . [Charles] Studd, waiting with his pads on, felt so cold that he asked the Surrey secretary for a blanket. With this wrapped around him he marched up and down the committee room in nervous agitation, still shivering with cold.

One of the 20,000 spectators at the ground had already died that afternoon. George Spendler haemorrhaged at the end of Australia's second innings, was carried into the pavilion – to be examined by the Surrey president Dr Jones among others – and was pronounced dead, aged 47. The tension on this cold, grey afternoon had, according to legend, another man chewing through the handle of his umbrella. It was in these moments, surely, that Test cricket came alive and gripped imaginations for evermore. The outcome, for the first time towards the end of a Test match, was uncertain – and uncertainty is sport's essence. Who was going to win the match: England or Australia, the old country or new? Who was going to be the match-winner: the Champion or the Demon, Grace or Spofforth?

It was Spofforth, with his fertile mind, who broke the deadlock. Still believing that this thing could be done, he went over to Murdoch, a solicitor when he was not captaining Australia. Spofforth proposed that England should be given a single so that the batsmen would change ends and he could bowl at Lyttelton. He did not concede the single himself, of course: Spofforth when in the mood did not concede anything. It was to be Boyle who conceded the single, and so it was that, after twelve consecutive maidens, Bannerman at mid-off misfielded and allowed Lyttelton to switch ends to face Spofforth. (This has become the accepted version, as much on Spofforth's egocentric testimony as anything, although Bannerman could have misfielded because of his finger injury.) Six wickets still left and, once the single had been conceded, only 19 runs to play with: it was, if true, a gamble taken by the representatives of a country keen on gambling, as the other countries which then played cricket – South Africa and the U.S.A. – were not.

Now it was Spofforth against Lyttelton. But the batsman knew the code, and played out two more Spofforth maidens. Boyle bowled two more maidens too, this time at Lucas. Five o'clock had come and gone; so had Mr Spendler. Seventeen consecutive four-ball overs had been bowled in which only 1 run had been scored. It was like watching a tightrope walker stuck halfway across the Niagara Falls, waiting to find his balance and nerve to go on.

At last the deadlock was broken, and Lyttelton's wicket, when Spofforth hit the top of his middle stump. England's score was 66 for five: only 19 to win, and five wickets left; but one end was open at last, and a new batsman had to adjust to the poor light. The advantage which England had held all through the game, except during Massie's innings, had gone. Next man in was Allan Steel. If his teeth were still chattering, he must have been reassured when Lucas cut Boyle for four, his first scoring stroke for almost an hour, and only his second in all after an early single.

Steel had been promoted by Hornby from number nine to seven on the strength of making 14 in his first innings – and his general, all-round excellence. Steel had hit Boyle over the top, and his captain might have hoped for something similar while Lucas blocked, but before Steel could take on Boyle he was caught-and-bowled by Spofforth. It could have been such a dismissal that Murdoch had in mind when he wrote of his star bowler: 'I have seen him take the same run, go through the same action, and to all appearances bowl with exactly the same strength as the previous ball; but, when the batsman played forward, he was much too soon.'

Fifteen runs to win, four wickets left. England clung to the knowledge that Maurice Read, William Barnes and Charles Studd, as well as Lucas, could all bat, even if Peate could not. Studd, who had been demoted to number ten, had scored two first-class hundreds already against the Australians that summer. Indeed the minimum number of centuries which ten members of this England side scored in their first-class careers was seven by Lyttelton. An England defeat was still inconceivable on paper, albeit long before conceived in the mind of Spofforth.

Read, the Surrey professional, not to be confused with the amateur Walter Read of the same county, was cheered to the wicket by his home crowd. In his first innings he had scored 19 not out, the second-highest score. He had also been hit in the ribs and on the elbow by Spofforth. Immediately Read was bowled – by Spofforth. England 15 to win, three wickets left. This thing could be done.

Spofforth tried a yorker first ball at Barnes. The Nottinghamshire all-rounder dug it out and the ball squirted away for 2. Spofforth's next ball beat Blackham as well as Barnes and went for 3 byes: only 10 runs to win now, three wickets left. Barnes came seventh in the national batting averages that summer, and scored three hundreds, one of them at the Oval against Surrey, so he was toothless in the literal sense alone. He had a high grip on the bat and liked to play what contemporaries called 'a forcing game'. Moreover, Barnes was the type of batsman whom Spofforth disliked even more than usual in that he had a two-eyed stance. Grace and Arthur Shrewsbury, soon to be acknowledged as the best professional batsman in England, had open stances too; Spofforth had worked out that such batsmen saw the ball more clearly than 'classical', side-on players, who restricted their own vision when they cut. No wonder Spofforth's biographer, Richard Cashman, called him 'the first thinking fast bowler'.

Barnes was facing Boyle though, and played out a maiden. Lucas of Essex faced Spofforth, as strokelessly as ever. A later photograph of Alfred Perry Lucas, who was a sound enough batsman to pass 10,000 first-class runs, cannot disguise a lugubrious expression behind the moustache. In those sporting days individuals were very seldom singled out for criticism, but when in its review of the Oval Test the *Sportsman* blamed the England batsmen for playing Spofforth and Boyle like 'so many tailors' dummies', Lucas with his fatal passivity was the most obvious target. When he inside-edged Spofforth on to his stumps, Lucas had played two scoring strokes and presided over England's decline from 53 for three, when he went in, to 75 for eight.

Spofforth had now taken fourteen of the eighteen England wickets to fall. He had taken the last four wickets – Lyttelton, Steel, Read and Lucas – for 2 runs in three overs. 'We all felt we were on top' he said in an interview with the *Cricketer* in 1921. But the truth is that still nobody knew what the outcome would be. Barnes and Studd could have knocked off the 10 runs in an over from Boyle without any need for Peate, who had once worked in a circus and batted like a clown.

Barnes was now facing up in the fading light to the first ball of Boyle's next over. No run. Boyle's second ball was climbing from the cut-up turf, hitting Barnes on the glove and lobbing to Murdoch closing in from point. Out! Ten runs still to win, 9 to tie, only one wicket left. Peate was joining Studd, who had yet to face a ball. And it is true, as tradition has it, that the hand of England's scorer had become so shaky that the last man's name looks in the scorebook to this day like Geese, not Peate. Filling the book with crosses, which marked a four-ball maiden, unlike the capital M of modern times, had not been enough to keep the scorer warm on that autumnal afternoon.

Two balls of Boyle's over were left. Peate was lashing out at the first, hoicking it to leg: it is said Yorkshire's left-arm spinner had already been at the champagne which had been prepared for England's victory. Peate was coming back for a second run, making it only 8 to win, and one ball of the over left before Studd could take strike against Spofforth. Peate was hoicking again at his second ball, the fourth and last ball of Boyle's over, and was bowled. Australia had won their first Test match in England by 7 runs.

The crowd was rushing on to the Oval field, as they were to do on so many future occasions in the history of the Ashes. They were trying to clap Spofforth on the back and shake his hand, then hoist him aloft and carry him to the pavilion. They were crowding in front of the pavilion and calling out the names of the Australian heroes in turn, so that each one had to come and present himself: Massie! Murdoch! Boyle, who had taken five wickets! Blackham, who had stood up on a difficult pitch for most of the match, made four dismissals and conceded only 9 byes! And, above everyone else, Spofforth, the Demon himself, who had bowled throughout: 43.1 six-ball overs in modern terms, taking fourteen wickets for 90, the best figures in Test history to this point, beating the thirteen wickets for 110 by Spofforth himself, naturally. There was no official Man of the Match, but then there was no need for one. He, almost alone, had thought it could be done, and did it.

The England players were crowding into the Australian dressing-room, shaking hands and sharing the champagne which they had blithely thought they had earned. An Australian player, under the pseudonym of 'One of the Team' in the *Argus* of Melbourne, said he would never forget these scenes of

> the tremendous throng in front of the pavilion (and their) multitudinous shouts of 'Bravo, Australians', 'Well done, boys' and so on . . . Then, when we were leaving the ground, how the crowd around our conveyance cheered us to the echo; how they almost took Spofforth off his legs in their desire to pat him on the back and shake hands with him for his really superb efforts with the ball; how the ladies from the windows in the Kennington-road waved their handkerchiefs to us, and how all the way back to Tavistock (the team hotel) the passers-by looked at us as if we had done something to make us famous for all time.

Looking back in his dotage, Greenwood summed it up as the best-placed, and most informed, and most objective witness. He had played for Yorkshire for fourteen years before becoming an umpire, and after he had umpired he used to go and watch Yorkshire's matches – on foot, because he could not afford the train. He lived in Ossett and walked to Leeds, Bradford and Huddersfield to see his old county play – 'and I was going to set off on the Sunday night to walk to Sheffield to see the match with Sussex, but when I found that Ranji was not playing I did not go.' After watching and playing all this cricket, old Luke Greenwood said: 'I never saw such excitement in my life as the match produced when one English crack after another fell.'

*   *   *

Most of the press criticism was serious in tone and directed at England's batsmen for their defensive approach. Although Grace and Ulyett had hit out, England had still scored at only 2.1 runs per six-ball over. Some Australians had wondered if the heat was having a debilitating effect on them in the Colonies, as Anglo-Saxons and Irishmen who stayed at home were never exposed to such heat. The victory of the Australian sculler Ned Trickett of Melbourne in races on the Thames in the 1870s was the first sign that their race had not degenerated, the accomplishments of Spofforth and his fellow cricketers the second. Indeed, such was the fibre which the Australians had displayed at the Oval that the following verse appeared in the London *Punch*, raising a serious point:

> Well done, Cornstalks, whipt us
> Fair and square.
> Was it luck that tripped us?
> Was it scare?
> Kangaroo land's Demon, or our own
> Want of devil, coolness, nerve, backbone?

For a country which had painted a quarter of the world red with its imperial conquests and ruled the waves; which had Victoria on the throne not only as a Queen but Empress; and which had suffered no serious military setback for a generation, since the Crimean War, this was astonishing self-doubt. The representatives of England lacking coolness, nerve and backbone? These were the very qualities which the British prided themselves upon. The culture of Empire, popularised by novelists like G.A. Henty and Rider Haggard, was founded on attributes which made the colonisers morally superior to the colonised. When Lord Harris left Kent to become Governor of Bombay in the 1890s, he observed that native Indians would never be any good at cricket because they lacked 'Anglo-Saxon phlegm'.

The saving grace was that the Australians were not brown savages but Anglo-Saxon cousins, except perhaps for the middle-order batsman Tom Horan who had been born in Ireland. Any serious introspection was also diluted by the piece of humour which immediately became the most celebrated comment on the Oval Test of 1882. This was the mock obituary which appeared in the *Sporting Times* four days afterwards:

In Affectionate Remembrance
OF
ENGLISH CRICKET,
WHICH DIED AT THE OVAL
ON
29th AUGUST, 1882,
Deeply lamented by a large circle of sorrowing
friends and acquaintances.

R. I. P.

N.B.—The body will be cremated and the
ashes taken to Australia.

The author of this clever wit was Reginald Brooks, the son of an editor of *Punch*. He was 27 years old and had already sown the seeds of his self-destruction. A wastrel, even by the standards of sports journalists through the ages, he drank and he gambled. By the age of 34 he was dead of heart trouble, but his concept will not be forgotten.

For Brooks' obituary notice contained the essence of wittiness, being not only funny but original and topical. To say that English cricket had died at the Oval was obvious enough; to add that the body would be cremated and the ashes taken to Australia was original. Cremation had always been banned by the Anglican and Roman Catholic Churches, who insisted on a Christian burial, for a fee. Then in 1869 a movement began to revive what had been the general practice in Greek and Roman civilisation. The Medical International Congress in Florence that year had been addressed by two Italian professors urging cremation 'in the name of public health and civilisation'. In 1873 a model of a cremating apparatus, made by Professor Brunetti of Padua, was exhibited at the Vienna Exposition and attracted the attention of Sir Henry Thompson, Surgeon to Queen Victoria, who on his return home championed the cause.

In the *Contemporary Review* of January 1874 Thompson argued that cremation would be 'a necessary sanitary precaution against the propagation of disease among a population daily growing larger in relation to the area it occupied'. He assembled a group of supporters at his house in Wimpole Street and drew up the following declaration: 'We, the undersigned, disapprove the present custom of burying the dead, and we desire to substitute some mode which shall rapidly resolve the body into its component elements, by a process which cannot offend the living, and shall render the remains perfectly innocuous.' The list of signatories included not only Thompson and the famous novelist Anthony Trollope, but also Shirley Brooks, the editor of *Punch* – and father of Reginald.

A long battle had yet to be fought before the Christian monopoly of the dead was broken, a battle that was still raging in August 1882. The Cremation Society of England had been founded at this meeting in Wimpole Street in January 1874, and it set about consulting legal opinion to see if cremation could be performed legally. The opinion being favourable, and funds having been subscribed, the Cremation Society tried to buy some land in the Great Northern Cemetery in London, but the Bishop of Rochester refused to allow a crematorium on consecrated land. The Society however was able to buy an acre adjoining the cemetery in Woking; an Italian professor brought over his cremating apparatus; and in 1879 the body of a horse was cremated without any smoke or effluvia escaping from the chimney. The inhabitants of Woking nevertheless protested to the Home Secretary, who refused to allow the cremation of human remains without an Act of Parliament, and there the matter rested until 1882, while the Society tried to change public attitudes.

Whether Reginald Brooks, by airing the issue in *Sporting Times* at the beginning of September 1882, had a significant impact on the debate cannot be known. What is certain is that less than six weeks after the Oval Test, on 8 and 9 October 1882, one Captain Hanham of Blandford in Dorset cremated his wife and his mother in a crematorium that he had built on his estate. Public discussion was intense, but the Home Office had taken no action by the time that Hanham himself died a year later and was also cremated. If this left the legalities in limbo, it was resolved by the bizarre episode which began when Dr William Price, an 83-year-old eccentric, tried to cremate the body of his five-month-old son, whom he had christened Jesus Christ. Price, who claimed to be a Druid High Priest, was arrested and tried in Cardiff. In February 1884 the judge ruled that cremation was legal provided no nuisance was caused to others in the process. Ever since, the popularity of cremation has increased, and it is now practised by over half of the British population.

Reginald Brooks, as a sports journalist, could not have been so deep in his cups that he was unaware of Bligh's touring party, who were to sail for Australia little more than a fortnight after the Oval Test, in mid-September 1882: and who would therefore have the opportunity to win back the ashes of English cricket, mythical as they were, and bring them home. Twelve years after his tour, Bligh was asked by the *Cricket Field* how it had originated:

> It happened that several of the Cambridge team were leaving the University, Steel and the Studds and Alfred Lyttelton among them, and, as we knew that Lord Harris enjoyed his visit to Australia two years before, we thought it would be very good fun. As I was captain at the time, it was left for me to arrange matters, and I at once wrote off to Australia. When we were about to leave England, Punch (at least I think it was Punch) had some verses to the effect that English cricket had been cremated at the Oval when Murdoch's team beat England, and that we were going over to bring back the ashes.

Bligh was probably misled by the Brooks connection into thinking it was *Punch* rather than the *Sporting Times*.

While the majority of Bligh's team set off on 14 September the Australians had several more matches in England and Scotland, and on both coasts of the United States, before they reached home. (The strength of American cricket was centred on the east coast, mainly Philadelphia, before fading after the First World War, when pacier pastimes were desired.) English cricket may have died at the Oval, according to Brooks, but Bligh's young bucks were full of life, and the idea of recovering 'The Ashes' was rapidly catching on as an exciting quest. Once he was in Australia, Bligh said that he and his players had travelled 16,000 miles in order to play Spofforth on a dry pitch, unlike the Oval, and to 'beard the lion in his den'.

In accordance with universal custom, after the mourning – and cremation – life had to go on.

3
Bligh Spirits

The most powerful images in English and Australian cricket relate to the Ashes. The urn itself; the crowd pouring on to the Oval field at the end of a series against Australia to celebrate friend or foe; Don Bradman being cheered all the way to the wicket for his final Test innings in 1948; Ian Botham sweeping away the 1981 Australians at Edgbaston; the sheer joy at England regaining the Ashes in 2005 after the most humiliating, if not the longest, wait. Of the most powerful images in English cricket, only the Pavilion at Lord's, massive and serene, can equal the Ashes, being the game's bastion.

Another image in English cricket is historical but it still holds a residual power. The scene is one of the London railway stations, or else Tilbury docks, or Southampton; and the England cricketers may either be setting forth to Australia or returning home. Either way, the crowd is large and swelled by former England players who, equipped with trilbies and reminiscences, have come to say goodbye or welcome home. Isn't that Mr Jardine over there? That must be Jack Hobbs – Sir Jack to you! And again these pictures draw their power from being part of the Ashes continuum, the longest-standing tradition of international rivalry in team sport.

14 September 1882 saw a prototype of this scene enacted at Gravesend when the SS *Peshawur* of the Peninsular and Oriental Company prepared to sail. It was only the seventh time that an English cricket team had sailed for the Antipodes, and for all the excitements generated at the Oval a fortnight before by Australia's 7-run victory, it would be hyperbole to state that Bligh's men carried

the nation's hopes. Moreover, of the first England team to contest the Ashes, only seven members embarked on this day. Two of the four professionals, William Bates of Yorkshire and Richard Barlow of Lancashire, were engaged to represent the North of England in their match against the Australians which was to start this very day at Old Trafford. They, along with George Vernon, George Studd and Charles Leslie, were to set off a week later, allowing them to pack less hurriedly and to avoid the Bay of Biscay, then train to Brindisi in the heel of Italy and meet up with the others at Suez.

The Sixth Earl of Darnley, Bligh's father and President of MCC in 1849, had come to say goodbye. So had Charles Alcock, the Surrey secretary who had arranged the Oval Test of 1882 and the editor of the magazine *Cricket*. Lord Harris, who had helped Bligh to set this tour in motion, was not present in person at Gravesend but he had sent the gift of a portable table, which the captain was to find useful during the voyage for writing while on deck or playing cards. Telegrams were delivered to Bligh from well-wishers varying from Australians to R.D. Walker of the famous Southgate and Middlesex family. George Studd and Vernon came in person to send off the seven. Neither had been in the England XI at the Oval; nor had Leslie, the Oxford University captain of that summer. Yet, with these exceptions, Bligh's team was almost representative of the full strength of English cricket, or at least of those available to tour. W.G. Grace was missing, the Gloucestershire amateur being exorbitantly expensive: when he next toured Australia in 1891/92, Grace's fee – excluding lavish expenses – was £3,000, ten times more than that of the so-called professionals. Missing too was George Ulyett, who had done enough donkey-work on Lord Harris's tour and preferred a winter at home in Sheffield, practising to become a pub landlord. Some critics argued that Alfred Lucas was a loss when he dropped out of Bligh's touring party just before the ship set sail, for he had toured Australia with Harris's team; and the captain could certainly have done with a thirteenth playing member. But his defensiveness had done much to lose the Oval Test when he let Spofforth bowl and bowl without an attacking shot, and Bligh's team may have been better off without Lucas; and they were distinctly better off without Albert Hornby, who had captained at the Oval and whose impetuosity would have rocked a young team's boat.

From the outset Bligh led from the front, as he was to do in all matters off, if not on, the field. The seven players were all accommodated in first-class, both the five amateurs and the two professionals, William Barnes and Fred Morley of Nottinghamshire, and they ate together at the same dining table. A mark of Bligh's captaincy was this integration of the two classes, when Australian opinion had been coming to the conclusion that English touring parties only worked if they were composed either of amateurs or professionals, not a mixture of the two. Bligh, even at 23, had the sensitivity to create an air of harmony and avert confrontation. On the English tour of Australia four years later Barnes smashed his fist against a wall and missed several matches: he had been aiming at the head of the Australian batsman Percy McDonnell. Had Bligh been captain rather than Arthur Shrewsbury, whom Barnes did not respect (indeed he refused to bowl at all in one Test), it is less likely the argument would have come to blows.

The very selection of Barnes and Morley said a lot about Bligh. They had been two of the seven Nottinghamshire professionals who had gone on strike the year before, in 1881, over pay and conditions. When the Nottinghamshire secretary Captain Holden forbade the professionals to put together their own team to play Surrey, they asked for a five-month summer contract with a benefit after ten years in return for making themselves available for all Nottinghamshire fixtures. This was reasonable enough in the eyes of MCC, who employed five of the players – including Barnes and Morley – on their groundstaff; and when some of the 'rebels' were selected to play for the Players against the Gentlemen, MCC let them play, whereas Nottinghamshire wanted them banned. These demands were reasonable enough too in the eyes of Bligh, who picked Barnes and Morley for a trip on which no troublemakers would have been welcome.

It was appropriate therefore that Bligh had a cabin to the fore of the *Peshawur* as he set off on an expedition which demanded diplomatic leadership. And if he felt in need of comfort and support he had only to open the door of the next cabin and behold his star player, Allan Gibson Steel, whose moustaches twirled up cheerfully at each end. If Grace and Ulyett were still the best cricketers in England, Steel was soon to overtake Ulyett and make himself second only to 'The Champion'. Steel was so accustomed to glittering prizes that he was to become the only man ever to captain his side to victory in the fixtures of Rugby v Marlborough, Cambridge University v Oxford University, Lancashire v Yorkshire, Gentlemen v Players and England v Australia. 'Nat', as Bligh knew him, had been the leading player in the most successful university cricket team of all time, the 1878 Cambridge side, which won all eight of their first-class matches, including an innings victory over the Australians. A good egg, too: in his obituary *Wisden* was to record that Steel 'as a man was always cheery and he never made an enemy. Nothing made him lose his temper, and many a young cricketer was helped by him, and there never existed anybody of whom he was jealous either among his professional brethren at the Bar or in the cricket field.'

Most sports to which Steel had turned his hand in his young life – he was to celebrate his 24th birthday during the voyage – had turned to gold. Standing only 5ft 7½in tall, he had played rugby for Cambridge University, and with Bligh he had won his Blue at racquets, the pair defeating their Oxford University rivals by 60 points to 33. But it was as a cricketer that Steel had shone most luminously. He was only fifteen when he was selected to represent Marlborough against Rugby in their annual contest at Lord's (Rugby's captain was George Vernon), and his impact was immediate. The weekly magazine *Cricket* was moved to pronounce: 'it is hardly too much to say that never – "well, hardly ever" – has such promising batting been shown at Lord's by a cricketer of his age and size.' These public school matches at Lord's, like the Varsity match, were grand occasions in Victorian times. A fellow who had performed nervelessly in them was not going to find a Test match daunting, for even if the Test crowd was equally large, it would not contain so many of the nation's aristocracy. Any unruly mob of natives in the colonies could also be faced without a tremble of the upper lip.

But it was as a bowler that Steel made his mark at Cambridge, for in his first season for them and for Lancashire he recorded the finest figures that any bowler has ever achieved in an English first-class season. In 1878 Steel took 164 wickets at nine runs each, the only time a bowler has taken one hundred wickets for a single-figure average. His style of bowling might at first sound outdated in that his stock ball was a rather round-arm off-break, but it was clearly suited to the conditions of his day, and he also had some variety which would have been effective through the ages: for he mixed in leg-breaks, especially a slower one which was so insidiously tempting that he had many a batsman stumped. He was unable to play cricket regularly after Bligh's tour, as he became a solicitor in Liverpool, but he was still skilled enough – even as a part-timer – to take on the England captaincy in 1886 and win all three Tests of the home series against Australia. Overall, Steel's first-class batting average of 29 was more than double his bowling average of 13; while in his thirteen Tests, all against Australia, the ratio between his batting average of 35 and his bowling average of 20 has been subsequently matched only by Sir Garfield Sobers, Jacques Kallis and Imran Khan. To set against these strengths, however, Steel had a weakness which the other three all-rounders were never forced to experience.

In the 28-page diary that Bligh wrote during the voyage out, he noted in his opening paragraph that it was a calm but foggy journey down the Thames 'and meals taken without trepidation. Well impressed by ship. Steel and myself secured cabins to ourselves for voyage – right forward – only drawback vibration of wheel machinery and steps of officers on watch just over me.' On future voyages to Australia some of Bligh's successors as England's captain tended to mull obsessively over the cricket ahead and the characteristics of their men, but Bligh was neither Douglas Jardine nor Len Hutton. He preferred to observe his surroundings and the personalities of all those around him: 'both officers and passengers seem to be of the right sort.' He noted the motion of the ship, which increased in the notorious Bay; the quality of the material comforts ('cooking on board very fair'); and at stops along the way took an interest in the flora, especially local fruit, and fauna.

The great talking point on board would have been the fighting in Egypt, particularly as the *Peshawur* had to sail past this war zone. The newspapers on 14 September 1882 were filled with reports of a famous victory by Sir Garnet Wolseley and the British army at Tel-el-Kebir the previous day and the crushing of the revolt led by Arabi Pasha. The front page of *The Times* was, as a matter of course, devoted to advertisements; and some of Bligh's cricketers might have been distracted by the prospects for the St Leger at Doncaster later in the week, if not by news of the Mansion House relief fund to aid the famine in Iceland (not Ireland), to which the Prime Minister William Gladstone had donated £10. Otherwise the latest military victory, which ensured that the Suez Canal would be open to the *Peshawur*, must have been the topic of conversation. *The Times* editorial for that day can stand forever as a model of jingoism:

> The Cabinet which was called together yesterday met to receive the news of one of the most brilliant victories that have rewarded British valour in recent days, and the Ministers might congratulate themselves on an event which places beyond doubt the complete success of the policy which, with the full assent and confidence of the country, they have pursued with respect to the rebellion in Egypt. SIR GARNET WOLSELEY yesterday morning delivered the decisive blow to which all we have hitherto done in Egypt is merely the prelude. It is impossible to conceive an operation more successful and operated in a more masterly manner. The intrenchments [sic] in which ARABI put his trust, and which were in truth formidable enough to justify some confidence, were carried with brilliant courage by the British troops . . . In the end the battle was won in the good old-fashioned English style, at the point of the bayonet.

To flesh out the details, Wolseley's telegram to the Secretary of State for War, sent from Ismailia on 13 September, was published under 'Latest Intelligence'. In it the General revealed that Arabi's fortified position at Tel-el-Kebir had been held by 20,000 regulars and 6,000 Bedouin and irregulars. 'My force was about 11,000 bayonets, 2,000 sabres and 60 guns. To have attacked so strong a position by daylight with the troops I could place in line would have entailed very great loss. I resolved, therefore, to attack before day-break, doing the six miles that intervened between my camp and the enemy's position in the dark.'

Arabi's 'crime' was to have raised the cry of 'Egypt for Egyptians'. His country had long been part of the Ottoman Empire, but recently the French and British had moved in as well. The French had completed construction of the Suez Canal in 1869, of which the British would have no part because they thought it would give the French a quick back-door route to India. But when Khedive Ismail wanted to raise money by selling his shares in the Canal, the British government snapped them up. Meanwhile Arabi, born near Alexandria as one of the 'fellaheen' or peasants, and educated in the 'Mussulman' not European style, was voicing the growing resentment of his people. First he and his followers protested at the law that forbade Egyptian fellaheen becoming officers in the Egyptian army. They also succeeded in having Arabic replace Turkish as the language of the Egyptian government. They resented 'Dual Control' too: the process by which French and British administrators had assumed control of Egypt's finances in 1876 to protect their investment in the Canal, and had Khedive Ismail deposed by the Sublime Porte and replaced by his son Tewfiq. These foreign administrators had to be paid by the Egyptians, yet they did not have to pay local taxes, and were outside the jurisdiction of Egyptian law. Resentment grew to the extent that the French and British sent in warships during the summer of 1882, and the British (but not the French) shelled the once-great city of Alexandria. Arabi was by now the Minister for War and led the Egyptian troops at Tel-el-Kebir on 13 September – to defeat. The Khedive Tewfiq, preferring discretion to valour, dissociated himself from his people by holding a large dinner for the British top brass in Alexandria the following day.

Bligh's diary contains a reference later on to British military activities in Africa – nationalism was stirring in the Sudan under the Mahdi as well as in Egypt – but he makes no direct comment upon the war and certainly no endorsement of it. Jingoism is conspicuous by its absence from his diary, while more than one entry throws light upon his humanity. A letter home to his father in the second half of the tour showed he was no snob either. When he tells his father about the decisive Third Test in Sydney, he refers to the generous applause which his team received, by comparison with the angry mob's heckling which Lord Harris had provoked: 'The Sydney crowd are most enthusiastic about us and I think the much abused larrikin is really less to blame than the favoured few who sit in the pavilion.'

Bligh was too diffident to be a natural extrovert: it was not until 18 September, the fourth day of the voyage, that he found out the name of another gentleman on his dining table. But on the very first day he met a couple who were to have the most profound impact on his life: William and Janet Clarke. It was a coincidence that they and Bligh's cricketers were aboard the same ship, but a fortunate one because he happened to be president of the Melbourne Cricket Club, the hosts and organisers of Bligh's tour. In addition to being the club's president from 1880 to 1886, Clarke was much else besides, including the most materially successful man in Australia.

Clarke's father, also William, had emigrated from Somerset to Tasmania, built up farming interests, moved to the mainland and soon owned vast estates. When the father died he was a multi-millionaire by today's reckoning, and his son William could devote himself to refinement rather than farming. For a suitable mansion he built Rupertswood at Sunbury near Melbourne, with its own railway station for the use of high society. He became the first president of the Victorian Football Association, governor of the Colonial Bank of Australia (not a sinecure during the recession of the 1890s), and Grand Master of the Masonic Lodge in Victoria. He built the first women's college at an Australian university and named it Janet Clarke Hall after his wife. Their year in England did their career graphs no harm: after he had endowed the Royal College of Music with a Clarke Scholarship, and no doubt furthered his Masonic contacts, Queen Victoria awarded him the Baronetcy of Rupertswood, the first title bestowed upon a person born in Australia. Still Clarke gazes over Melbourne from the top of his monument in the public gardens, benevolent and bewhiskered.

On the first day Bligh noted that Clarke, very soon to be Sir

William, had 'a party of 16'. On the third day he 'made acquaintance with Mr Clarke's party including some funny little boys whom CTS is yarning to', CTS being Charles Studd. A tradition has it that Bligh also met his future wife on this voyage. Joy Munns, the locally-based historian of Rupertswood, states in her book *Beyond Reasonable Doubt*: 'It was during the voyage that Ivo Bligh was first introduced to Janet Clarke's companion, Florence Rose Morphy.' But a list of 90 first-class passengers, quoted by Ronald Willis in *Cricket's Biggest Mystery*, does not include the name of Florence Rose Morphy. It includes William and Janet Clarke, and two other Clarkes, and two Miss Alfords, who were being accompanied by the Clarkes. There was also a Lily Snodgrass, perhaps Janet's sister, for that was her maiden name. But no Miss Morphy in first-class, which she surely would have been as Lady Clarke's companion. Bligh's diary does not make any mention of a young lady catching his attention; and in a letter home during the tour he states that he has met Miss Morphy at her Rupertswood home and in Melbourne, without any reference to a shipboard introduction.

The tradition, however, is attractive enough to make us wish it were true. A breathless Janet picks up her skirts and hastens to Florence's cabin on making a discovery. There she confides in her impressionable companion that she has seen a most tall and elegant young Englishman, with a title to boot; and together they plot how Florence might meet him, preferably on deck on a moonlit night in the warm Mediterranean. Not for nothing were eligible girls going out to the colonies known as 'the fishing fleet'. Alas, though, this version of events cannot be confirmed.

Sunday 17 September saw Bligh attending the morning and evening service aboard ship, conducted by a clergyman, and the *Peshawur* sailing past Finisterre into calmer seas at an average of 12 knots. 'All party recovered completely bar self' wrote Bligh, in the first entry which speaks of his less than robust constitution. 'Sun very hot and doesn't suit back of my head, bathing establishment decidedly good.' Unlike later touring parties to Australia, this one had no physiotherapist or fitness trainer to keep the players in shape. Bligh observed: 'doesn't seem to be much chance of cricket on board as upper deck is small and main deck narrow.' Instead, his team played whist and 'quoits in the bucket' while the captain – unable to read before Gibraltar – contented himself with sightings of whales, porpoises and petrels.

Another passenger was the only journalist sent to cover Bligh's tour for the British press: Martin Cobbett, who was sent by the *Sportsman*, first-class too. He must surely have introduced himself to Bligh at the outset, for the captain tells his diary on the second day: 'a reporter Cobbett has come out to report for Sportsman – a good specimen of the class luckily for us' (not that Bligh had a bad word for anyone he knew). Such a good specimen was Cobbett that when Bligh's side was a man short for a match in Tasmania, he made up the numbers. Whereupon Cobbett, even if he was the first, was certainly not the last journalist to make the discovery that the standard of England's cricketers was infinitely superior to what he fondly imagined his own to be. When he played against XVIII of Northern Tasmania at Launceston, not the most demanding of fixtures, and went in at number eleven, Cobbett played such an expansive cut at his first ball that the point fielder ducked for cover, while the ball hit his leg stump and clean bowled him for nought.

After Bligh had returned from his expedition to Australia in the middle of 1883, his father was to write that Ivo looked much healthier than when he had left England. To the illness, physical or mental, which had kept him out of the 1882 first-class season, the motion of SS *Peshawur* and the sun added further discomfort. Even when he found the weather splendid, and he ventured 'a little extempore singing after dinner', the next day he felt 'rather tired and unwell still'. The ship's fog whistle gave him a bad night, not to mention the wheel machinery and the footsteps above his cabin. When a sports committee was formed, England's cricket captain served on the music committee. When he thought his health was 'getting better gradually', he fell out of bed – 'a rather painful adventure'. He does not, however, record with self-pity but in the same matter-of-fact style that he notes that Barnes was especially 'uncomfortable' in the Bay of Biscay; or that cricket was actually played on deck, one week out, after Malta; or that he 'played at proverbs in evening with Clarke party'. Bligh was not very hale and decidedly not hearty. The tone he set for his players – not that the Studd brothers needed it – was a kind and gentle one.

Smoking cannot have been good for his health, for he was to die of a heart attack, but in following the fashion of the day he bought cigarettes ashore in Malta – cheap at seven shillings and sixpence for 250 'and very fair smoking'. Bligh also took in the sights around Grand Harbour, while the *Peshawur* refuelled and coal dust was spread liberally, covering some cabins. Bligh's wicketkeeper Edward Tylecote went to the opera, not by himself or with another cricketer but in the company of Cobbett. 'New opera house very nice indeed.'

Nothing could better illustrate Bligh's humanity than his reaction when the *Peshawur* arrived in Port Said on 26 September 1882. He spent a morning inspecting the principal streets and found the town, as many a British traveller did, a 'very uninteresting place, indeed very hot and dusty'. But whereas many a British traveller found the natives to be a low, thieving bunch of rascals, the unprejudiced Bligh made quite the opposite judgement, in spite of all the jingoism that prevailed: 'Arabs far the finest men I have seen on the shores of the Mediterranean.' It is doubtful whether Ulyett, the Yorkshire all-rounder, passed the same judgment during the English tour to Australia two years later, when he and Alfred Shaw went ashore at Suez. On the way back to their ship Ulyett threw one of the two Arab oarsmen out of the boat, admittedly after the latter had tried the old trick of stopping halfway and demanding more money.

In the afternoon four of Bligh's men played cricket on the sands at Port Said, which gave them a foretaste of Australia at its most sweltering. For Bligh the heat was so intense that he tried to sleep at night on deck, and cooled himself by day with fruit. 'Better grapes to be had than at Malta and watermelons also pretty good. Very juicy but not the flavour of other melons.'

It was the Suez Canal which had put Australia within reasonable reach of English cricketers. Before 1869, the voyage via Cape Town took more than two months, which left little time for a profitable tour of Australia before returning home to take up a professional engagement in the next English season. The Canal cut the voyage to six weeks. The first English cricket tour – the first of all overseas cricket tours barring the one to France by the Duke of Dorset in 1789 which had to be cancelled – was to North America in 1859. The second, to Australia, was in 1861/62 and only one more followed before the Suez Canal was opened.

A long-standing tradition of English cricketers being entertained by British sailors was initiated – if it had not already begun – when the seven players, amateur and professional, were invited to breakfast on board the *Ruby* at Suez: 'most hospitably received by Captain Foot and officers, some of them being keen cricketers.' That evening – Sunday 2 October – they were no longer seven in number, for 'at 6 o'clock the long expected *Poonah* came in sight bringing our other 5 thank goodness all safe and sound.' The P and O steamship *Poonah* was accustomed to having cricketers on board as she had taken Jim Lillywhite's party to Australia in 1876/77.

Bligh told his diary that the new arrivals brought with them 'no particular news of the war except that an accident has happened to a train full of wounded.' But the passengers on the *Poonah*, including the cricketers, had seen for themselves the effects of the war, for on 28 September the *Poonah* had called at Alexandria. In his memoirs the senior professional Barlow recalled with the sympathy of an eyewitness, not the jingoism of an editorial-writer:

> Ours was the very first boat to call here after the war and the now historic bombardment of Alexandria. A few of our party went ashore for a few hours to see the effects of the bombardment. The havoc wrought by the shells and projectiles which were fired into the town from the guns of the 'Alexandra', 'Monarch', 'Invincible', 'Penelope', 'Condor', and other British vessels, baffles description. The buildings were completely wrecked, and the place a heap of ruins.

Thus was the city which had been the mother of western science in its Greek period reduced by British warships to rubble.

The five arrivals also brought news of the defeat of the Australians by the North of England, for whom Barlow and Bates had played, at Old Trafford. Is there a Freudian connection between the two parts of this sentence separated merely by a colon in Bligh's diary? 'Heard news of defeat of Australians at Manchester by North of England by 10 wickets: one or two sharks seen in harbour.'

The *Peshawur* made around 300 miles per day through the Red Sea and the pace of life was relatively brisk for a while. 'The Peshawur Gazette has been published with fair success' reported Bligh, whose experience on the school magazine at Eton no doubt came into play. The new publication contained 'an article on deportment addressed to young men and women'. The pace slowed as the ship headed almost due south. 'Horrid damp heat the whole time, day and night.' The thermometer fluctuated, but only from 90°F to 96°F in the shade. 'Everyone self included wilting, done up in the heat. Heavy dew at night making sleep on deck uncomfortable if not dangerous.'

A change occurred, if not much for the better, when the *Peshawur* encountered what Bligh thought was the monsoon, although it resembled a thin Scotch mist which made everything sticky. Blessed relief came with some cooler weather as they approached Colombo, and Bligh found the energy to read Anthony Trollope's two-volume book about Australia, concluding it was 'a most useful guide'. Trollope had highlighted the Australian habit of 'blowing' or making superlative claims about the country, and Bligh had already heard the book had not been well received there.

Ceylon was their next stop. It was to be the next stop too of Arabi Pasha, after he had been tried and sentenced to death, only for his sentence to be commuted to exile in Ceylon. (He was allowed to return to Egypt in 1901, with still half a century to go before Egyptians were free to rule their own country.) In Colombo the secretary of the local cricket club – European, of course – came aboard and arranged a match between Bligh's team and XVIII of Colombo, to commence at midday. Before then the players had time to go ashore, stretch their legs and pursue their individual bents. Bligh, Steel and the two Studds, George and Charles, were taken to a bungalow where they were to spend the night, while the rest of the party were put up at the club. This bungalow belonged to a man whom Bligh does not name and does not identify in any way, other than he was a Christian. When the touring party had to return perforce to Colombo, these four players – the four Cambridge contemporaries – again went and stayed with this Christian. While there was horse-play at the club involving some of the other cricketers, none appears to have taken place at the bungalow.

Bligh and Steel were to spend the rest of their lives in secular society; the brothers Studd were to become noted, even famed, as missionaries. At this stage of their lives, just down from Varsity, they were still searching. George was the elder, and had succeeded Bligh as Cambridge captain in 1882; Charles was the younger and more brilliant on the cricket field. Indeed, not only had he been the one batsman to score two first-class centuries against the Australian tourists of that summer, he had also taken more than a hundred wickets with his medium-pace, thus becoming only the second all-rounder to do the double after W.G. Grace. The brothers had been born in Northamptonshire, grew up at Tedworth House in Wiltshire, and were sent to Eton by a father who had amassed a large fortune in India before retiring to England. Already, in the late 1870s, their father had been converted to born-again Christianity. His sons, the two brothers, had not as yet been persuaded, but Bligh's diary shows how close to conversion they already were.

Having arrived in the early morning, and gone to this Christian's house for breakfast, Bligh and his three friends arrived at the ground for a 12 o'clock start. Around a thousand people 'of every variety of colour in dress and complexion' watched the local Europeans bat first, after winning the toss, and put up a total of 92. Barlow recalled: 'The team we played against included several hardy fellows, who batted in their bare feet and wore neither pads nor other protection.' All of the English bowlers had a turn, while Tylecote's wicket-keeping was 'very good and all the fielding throughout very smart' according to Bligh. The benefits of having a young team, Tylecote being the oldest at 33, were immediately apparent.

By the close of this opening day of Bligh's tour his players had scored 79 for four wickets in reply. When the game resumed next morning at quite possibly the earliest hour any England cricket team has played a match, 8 a.m., the professionals Bates and Barnes carried on their overnight innings and steered their team to 150. Some of them were sunburnt from the previous afternoon's play, but they were finding their landlegs, and by 11 a.m. they had reduced the locals to 18 for six wickets in their second innings. At this point stumps were drawn and breakfast was taken, as the *Peshawur* was due to sail at three in the afternoon, dusty again from refuelling. Morley did not play in this game – he had been suffering from a weak ankle during the English season – and neither did Bligh, although he felt well enough to give a speech of thanks to the club for their hearty welcome. He was not quite a passenger in the touring party in playing terms, but a passenger from the *Peshawur*, one Charles James, fielded for him.

*   *   *

The Ashes came close to never existing. Bligh and his team nearly drowned in the middle of the Indian Ocean. Or the ashes could have been the remains of real, cremated, cricketers.

It hit them as suddenly as a realisation. The *Peshawur* was steaming at 12–13 knots in a position 580 kilometres from Colombo at 9.13 p.m. on 15 October 1882. The more devout passengers were on deck as Captain Edward Baker of the *Peshawur* had just finished reading the evening service. Several players were still pacing the decks, while Cobbett – none too surprisingly for a journalist – was in the bar. (Alas, the days had gone when P and O allowed free drinks for the whole voyage to first-class passengers.) Suddenly Baker ordered the engines to reverse and go full speed astern. The captain had seen something emerge out of the darkness. Barlow later gave his doubtless sober testimony to the court of inquiry in Colombo: 'I was standing by the saloon door, looking over the ship's side. I saw something in sight – a dark object and no light. A minute or two later, I turned round to see if any of our cricketers were about, to tell them about this something in sight.'

While Captain Baker shouted urgent orders, the other captain – Bligh – watched so alertly he was able to set down later in his diary a lucid account of what happened, one not too complicated by nautical terms:

> Just after evening service about 9 o'clock, the engines were suddenly reversed and a red light was seen bearing down on us on our starboard side. We all assembled on the quarter deck, went to the side to look at what we thought was a stationary vessel possibly signalling to us in distress. The light got nearer and nearer and in about a minute we could hear loud shouts going on across the water from their vessel. Even then no idea of danger entered our heads till all in a moment there loomed out of the darkness a large ship right upon us coming at an angle . . . The whole crowd went helter skelter across the deck falling over each other and everything else, all possessed with but one idea in that sudden death was both upon them and those dear to them. The ladies on the whole kept wonderfully cool. Almost directly we had left the side a fearful crash told us that the vessel was into us and then for some seconds we heard the sickening sounds of great iron plates, bars and spars torn off in all directions like matchwood . . . The vessel ground her way along us and disappeared after taking away with her three of our boats. The utmost alarm prevailed for some time as the very general idea shared also by the officers was that we must sink in a few minutes. On clearing away the debris however it was found that although there was an enormous hole in our side only very little damage was done below the line of the main deck.

It would have been appropriate had the Polish-born novelist Joseph Conrad been aboard the ship which had rammed the *Peshawur*. The *Glenroy* was the creation of an empire which voraciously demanded manual labour at cheap cost, uprooting people and transporting them to where their hands were wanted. She was an iron ship, 25 years old and a little over a thousand tons; an English ship coming from Mauritius, bound for Madras then Calcutta. Her cargo was coolies: 400 of them, according to the *Glenroy*'s quartermaster when he shouted after the collision to Captain Baker, or 500 by Bligh's account. The *Glenroy*'s captain, John Wright, was subsequently found guilty of not displaying the necessary green light on the starboard side, and of displaying the red light on the port side only minutes before the collision. Wright's punishment was to have his certificate suspended for six months.

Fortunately, only two people on the *Peshawur* were seriously injured, and at the time their number was thought to be one. This was a 'native' – or a Lascar, as Bligh preferred to dignify him – whose job was to supply the ship's bar with ice. Cobbett, in the bar rather than at the service, picked him up after the collision. This may not have been the wisest course of action because the unfortunate man had his leg broken in two places by falling debris, as the two doctors on board soon found. Bligh observed: 'The bar man had a miraculous escape as the bar was completely smashed up.' In addition to the gaping hole in the *Peshawur*'s side, the decks were covered in rubble from the *Glenroy*'s bow, which had disintegrated on impact. Another *Peshawur* passenger was to recall: 'an immense quantity of stones, bricks and mortar were strewn about, this being the cement from the bows of the other ship.'

The *Glenroy* was in a worse condition. She would surely have sunk with all hands if the *Peshawur* had not been in a position to help, or if the night had been stormy instead of perfectly calm. Captain Baker ordered his ship to spend the rest of the night circling the *Glenroy* protectively until dawn offered a full picture of the damage which her negligent captain had caused. The *Glenroy*'s bow had been completely shot away and she was making water through her foremost watertight bulkhead. The *Peshawur* had no humane option but to tow this broken vessel back to Colombo, as the only other land within several hundred miles was the Chagos Islands, which had not yet been taken by the U.S.A. and turned into a military base. Hawsers were fastened from ship to ship, but they kept breaking. Not until the afternoon was the *Peshawur* to begin towing, when Bligh noted: 'We could see as many as 20 or 30 sharks swimming round and round the ships. They tried fishing for them and got 2 or 3 – one half way up the side of the ship but there they stopped – he wriggled off again.'

Otherwise, the towing back to Colombo was uneventful, even tedious, for the passengers on the *Peshawur* if not the tramp steamer, causing as it did severe disruption to Bligh's itinerary in Australia.

We tried seven knots at first but the big hawser broke at once, then 5 which lasted for some hours with 2 wire hawsers – then we had to slow down as the *Glenroy* is making water fast and they have to pump with all hands . . . The several hawsers that have broken have all done so near the other ship luckily for us or some painful accident must have happened. Many of the passengers rashly sitting or walking all round hawser.

A solicitous captain, Bligh, on land and sea. Gallant enough too not to record for posterity the name of the cricketer who, immediately after the collision, omitted to bear in mind the convention of women and children first. 'One of our team was observed it is said with 2 lifebuoys under his arm ready for the worst, another with a young ladies' [sic] arms round his neck.'

However in a letter home to his father at the end of the tour, when recalling this incident, Bligh said there had been no serious exception to his team behaving well after the collision. Which had not been the case when the second English touring team to Australia in 1863/64 had been involved in a collision at sea. The team, under their captain George Parr of Nottinghamshire, were on their way from Sydney to Melbourne when their ship struck another ship, which sank almost immediately. Parr was reported to have been 'paralysed with alarm', while his fast bowler George Tarrant reacted with the most inappropriate behaviour, running around to collect his valuables then trying to jump into the lifeboat which had been lowered to pick up the passengers of the sinking ship.

Once the *Peshawur* had towed the *Glenroy* as far as Galle, Cobbett went ashore in order to go by coach and train to Colombo, there to file his exclusive story by telegraph. Arrived in Colombo, while the *Peshawur* was being repaired, Bligh and his Cambridge contemporaries returned to the unnamed Christian's bungalow where, in their iron beds, they were safe from the lightning brought by the north-east monsoon. Bligh telegraphed to Australia to advise the Melbourne Cricket Club of the delay. He also arranged a match against XVIII of the garrison for the following day, a Monday.

Early that morning he went for a drive '4 in hand' down the coast to the Mount Lavinia hotel and was pleased by its location. On

Monday afternoon the Fusiliers of the garrison proved themselves to be unskilled at cricket. 'We went in, and scored 180. Tyley 45 GB 35 (self 9). They got 22 for 9 wickets. Stopped several times by rain. Bates and Morley got the wickets.' It was the captain's first innings of the tour, his first of note since the 1881 season.

Once the repairs had been made, and the court of inquiry had heard the evidence from passengers and crews, the *Peshawur* left Colombo for the second time on Tuesday 24 October and was soon full speed ahead. Bligh's diary is notable for its moderation of tone, its kindliness, but not in the following entry: 'One night passed 2 sailing ships <u>without lights</u>, hanging too good for the captains of these ships. Had to alter our course for both of them. Look-out as usual tremendously sharp at night and as this proves not without a reason.'

If this language is strong – 'hanging too good' – the collision had an effect upon him which seems to have been traumatic to some degree. By the time the *Peshawur* had towed the *Glenroy* back to Colombo, Bligh had written a long poem about the accident. The poem runs to three pages and nineteen stanzas of four lines apiece. Even if the standard of Victorian verse about transport accidents is not high, it is a commendable effort for an occasional amateur, a sincere attempt to come to terms with the shock. The last two stanzas indicate that his extra work on his classical verses at Eton had not been in vain, and constitute the pick:

> So we retire a sobered throng
> And thankful lips that night
> Poured forth to our Creator great
> Their prayer for that great might
>
> That saved us and our dear ones
> From the cold ocean wave
> Which but for this almighty power
> To us had proved a grave.

It was the first time that Bligh consigned profound emotions in poetry to his diary, but not the last.

The rest of the voyage to Australia passed none too comfortably but without serious incident. Barlow noted that 'for several days, the sea was very rough, preventing many of the passengers from going below for meals.' Nothing more was recorded in Bligh's diary after a two-line entry for the day after they had left Colombo. And it was written in a different, less assured hand than hitherto, and clearly some time after the event: 'Wednesday 25: Hurt my hand badly in tug of war. Arm in a sling up to day of landing in Melbourne.'

In the report which Bligh was to write on the tour for *Lillywhite's Cricketers' Annual*, he amplified slightly on this accident. He noted that his 'hand had been rather severely cut on board ship'. It is difficult to imagine how anybody could get injured in a sociable tug-of-war, unless Bligh was the man at one end of the rope, had it wound too tightly around his wrist and was dragged forwards across the deck when the other side won; but out of action he was, again, and for several weeks. In a later letter home to his father, he said that his lack of runs in Australia was due to his missing the 1882 season and to his injured right hand. His players must have been rather dismayed to find their captain was *hors de combat* after one brief game in Colombo.

The voyage in all events was not so rough as some touring parties have known. By the start of the twentieth century, P and O ships like the *Orontes* could sail at 18 knots without rolling, save in the stormiest seas: the captain of the 1903/04 side to tour Australia, Plum Warner, called her 'a veritable palace of comfort'. Nineteenth-century passengers like Bligh's touring party were not so blessed. On the voyage out on the 1878/79 tour, Tom Emmett overcame his seasickness to the extent of venturing on deck, where the captain Lord Harris was smoking a cigarette. 'Glad to see you out, Tom, but you don't look very well' said his lordship. 'Noah, me Lord' Emmett replied, 'Ah doant feel very broight.' The Yorkshire all-rounder surveyed the turbulent waves. 'Ah doant think they've 'ad the 'eavy roller on, me Lord.'

Ten days behind schedule, the *Peshawur* arrived at Adelaide, off Glenelg. It was the night of 9 November 1882. In almost two months they had travelled halfway across the world, seen sharks and whales, visited Port Said and Suez, Colombo and (in the case of some of Bligh's party) Kandy, suffered a collision and narrowly avoided at least two more. And in this period the cricketers had bonded, unwittingly, whereas England players today have to go for a specific bonding session – paintballing perhaps – before flying off by air. They were breaking new ground in being a mixed party, of amateurs and professionals in some proportion, and they made it work by travelling first-class together and by taking their meals together. When the five who had gone overland joined them at Suez, the other seven moved to a larger table so they could eat as a team. It was not especially comfortable – 'we sit right over the screw, cool but noisy, not good in time of bad weather' – but it seated all twelve of them.

Another element in their unity was that no wives or womenfolk accompanied them. W.G. Grace had used the 1873/74 tour as a honeymoon for himself and his wife Agnes. By 1903/04 Plum Warner was taking his fiancée, also called Agnes, as well as his players. The captain of English touring parties has always had greater freedom in these matters than ordinary players, but seldom can team spirit have been enhanced when the captain alone has been accompanied by his wife.

And the very time which the players spent together under the kindly eye of their young captain was sufficient not only to rest them after the rigours of the English season, but also to give them the strength and team spirit to carry them through their tour to victory: of only twelve subsequent England cricket teams to Australia can that be said. During this voyage these players were united under their 23-year-old captain. They became, so to speak, Bligh spirits.

4
A Quick Catch

It must have been louder and more startling than the noise which raised the Porter in *Macbeth*. It might even have reminded the English cricketers of their collision with the *Glenroy*, such was the commotion. There they were, fast asleep in their cabins in the *Peshawur* anchored off Adelaide in the early hours of Friday 10 November 1882, when the noise began.

Bligh's diary entry for that day was, understandably, a bit blurry. His account for *Lillywhite's Cricketers' Annual*, written after the event, was much more lucid.

> The feelings of the team generally, and the perplexity of the captain in particular, may be imagined when, at the hour of 2.30 a.m., they were hastily aroused from their slumbers to receive a deputation of some twenty gentlemen who, fortified by a dinner given that night by the Mayor in honour of the Prince of Wales' birthday, had resolved to welcome the team at whatever hour they arrived.

If Bligh had not already realised he was in Australia, he did now.

Bligh and his players were late, ten days late owing to the *Glenroy*: that same Friday was due to have been the second day of the first match of their tour, against XV of South Australia. Nevertheless, it was a rude awakening for them, if not intentionally so. Indeed it is none too difficult to reconstruct the scene. At this fortifying dinner to celebrate the royal birthday, a member of the welcoming committee has had a bright idea. He has then proposed it to Mr Peacock, the head of this committee. 'Hey, Peaky, how about we go and stir up those Poms and buy 'em a drink? Let's go over to the *Peshawur* now and buy that bloody Bligh – beg your pardon, the Honourable bloody Bligh – a few beers. He's probably never had a decent beer in his honourable little life. My oath, this gangplank is wobbling a bit! Hey, g'day mate, you must be the captain who's come out here to get beaten. Whadya mean, you wanna sleep? You've just had two bloody months to sleep. Wait till Spofforth starts bowling at yer – that'll wake yer up!'

Bligh's diary mentions some 'ineffectual attempts' to stem this deputation and their offers of hospitality. His report for *Lillywhite's* recounts with a trace of irony:

> When our good friend, Mr Peacock, proceeded to explain to the half-awakened cricketers that a special train was actually awaiting them on shore, and that a match that day (Friday) was confidently looked forward to by the many thousands assembled in the town, it was evident that our contemplated refusal to play on the plea of want of practice – surely not a fanciful one – would cause great disappointment; and so, though a more decent time for disembarking – nine o'clock next morning – was fixed upon, the demands of Mr Peacock's deputation were in the main acceded to.

'A very gloomy party we were too' Bligh confided to his diary, as the cricketers left their ship later that morning. Not simply because of their disturbed sleep and the demand to play cricket as soon as they had landed, but because they had to say goodbye to the *Peshawur*. 'It is in all probability the most eventful voyage any of us will ever make and certainly with all its mishaps on the whole a wonderfully pleasant one. It really was harder than leaving home so attached had we become – but now our trip through the colonies really at last about to commence.'

The special train took them from Glenelg to the centre of Adelaide. (Their predecessors of 1876/77, Jim Lillywhite's team, had to go by coach and horse.) There Bligh and Tylecote were whisked off to stay at Government House with Sir William Jervois, while the other amateurs were put up at the South Australian Club. The amateurs and professionals were quartered in the same hotels in some country towns but in the larger cities they stayed separately, amateurs at a club, professionals at a hotel, which occasioned the odd comment in the egalitarian Australian press. However, the South Australian Club would not have felt like a home from home for Barlow, Barnes, Bates and Morley: so stiff and starchy, it did not deign to serve anything so vulgar as Australian wine until after the Second World War. The four professionals were quartered at the Prince Alfred hotel. The 1876/77 English tourists had stayed at the Globe Hotel in Rundle Street, which had claimed to have the widest range of liquors in the colony.

Between showers – outdoor showers – Bligh's team were allowed a morning's practice at the Adelaide Oval in which to find their legs, their length, and the middle of their bats, before the match began after lunch. A grandstand had been constructed specifically for Bligh's visit, and it helped to accommodate 7–8,000 spectators on the second day, the biggest crowd for a cricket match that the city had seen. Adelaide was a junior relation to her fellow free-settler city of Melbourne, and her citizens were naturally keen to welcome the English cricket team in their first port of call and put Adelaide on the map. The city had been founded only 45 years before by Captain Light, on the River Torrens.

Bligh told his diary:

> Very much pleased with the appearance of the town, prettily situated . . . The usual wide streets and somewhat unfinished appearance of large buildings with great spaces between them. The ground a very fine one – oval in shape, 300 yards long by about 250. Very fast and good wicket. Rain fell heavily in the morning and again later so as to stop play and the prepared wicket was rejected in favour of another, which at first played a bit bumpily but next day very well indeed. We made a bad-ish start and when the rain came down had lost six wickets for 66 – Barnes and Tyley not out.

At least it was rain which had halted play: at a match in Adelaide on the next English tour in 1884/85 the players had to throw themselves to the ground to avoid being suffocated by a dust storm.

As in Colombo, Tylecote acted as captain in the absence of Bligh.

The oldest member of the party, he was in every sense a safe pair of hands, except perhaps when it came to romance. 'Tyley' had been educated at Clifton College in Bristol, where he had been in the first XI for five years, before going to Oxford University where he finished as captain. Clifton is famous for having seen the highest individual innings ever played in a formal match, the innings of 628 not out by Arthur Collins in a junior house match in 1899. But Collins was not the first Clifton boy to set a world record for the highest innings. Tylecote had done the same in his time at the school: in a game between Classical and Modern in the year 1868 he had scored 404 not out, the first quadruple-century on record. The school archives contain so much material that nobody has yet managed to unearth the details of Tylecote's innings, whereas photocopies of the original scorecard of Collins' innings are prominently displayed. But it is possible that Tylecote made his huge score on the same ground as Collins, the ground which is still known in his memory as 'Collins', with its stone-wall boundaries of no more than 30 yards to either side of the wicket. After Oxford, where he became a maths tutor, Tylecote was brought into the Kent side by Lord Harris, even though Kent had a perfectly capable wicketkeeper in Harry Wood, a professional, who had to move to Surrey.

On their first evening in Adelaide the English team dined with the Governor ('most of the swells there' Bligh observed). In the pre-television age the occasion of an England team visiting Australia, or vice versa, was an excuse for many speeches, dinners and toasts – as in India or Pakistan, without the toasts, in more recent times. Bligh could not let his diary entry pass without reference to a slight faux pas at this reception. It was probably made by one of his four professionals, but there is nothing condemnatory in the captain's tone, which is if anything affectionate. 'One of the team is reported in the innocence of his heart to have asked the Prime Minister whether he was interested in politics!' Morley might be a good guess, as he was said to have been a simple soul, civil and unassuming, or Barnes after a couple of stiffeners; and it might not have been a stupid question at all, but a very wise one, in that some leaders are interested in power, not politics.

Tylecote the next morning fathered a recovery from the embarrassment of his team's overnight position. Some spectators on the first day may have made little allowance for the tourists' lack of practice – and of sleep – and declared there was nothing to write home about. Tylecote and Barnes began to show English cricket in a much better light as the pitch dried out and they became accustomed to Australian conditions, taking the score up to 135 before being separated. Tylecote was dropped several times, his '59 rather lucky but most useful and plucky innings and under the circumstances a wonderfully good one. Barnes 42 played very well.' This was one of the few occasions the Nottinghamshire all-rounder excelled on his first tour of Australia, where he seems to have been seduced by what Cicero called 'the familiar comforts'.

After Bligh's team had scored 153, six of his bowlers had a turn, of ten to twenty overs apiece, four-ball overs as in England. Most surprisingly, in view of what transpired, Morley, in Bligh's opinion, was the pick of them with three of the seven wickets which fell as South Australia scored 128 before the close. Jesse Hide, the former Sussex professional, was groundsman at the Adelaide Oval and opened the batting, if not successfully on this occasion, but he did fine work for South Australian cricket in general. Hide had been recommended by Jim Lillywhite when the local association asked for a county cricketer to come out from England to act as groundsman at the Adelaide Oval and coach. So rapidly did Hide raise the standards, even though South Australia always lacked the population of New South Wales and Victoria, that the son of the coachman who had driven Lillywhite's players from Glenelg to Adelaide in 1876/77 became Australia's finest left-handed batsman before the First World War, Clem Hill.

However, in 1882 Hide had not been in his post for long and the standard of South Australian batsmanship was still poor. Bligh was able to find something to praise, though, writing in *Lillywhite's* that 'on Noel and Giffen becoming partners some really good cricket was shewn, both batsmen combining good defence with resolute, clean hitting on the off side . . . Noel also proved himself to be a very fine field, and should be a useful candidate for a place in the next

Australian eleven.' Noel was to be given no such opportunity, but Walter Giffen was to be given a tour of England in 1886, if only because of his elder brother. At this time George Giffen was on the way back from the 1882 tour of England and towards becoming the finest all-rounder that Australia has ever produced in terms of first-class figures, still the only Australian to have scored 10,000 runs and taken 1,000 wickets.

*   *   *

Bligh and his team had arrived at Adelaide in the early hours of the Friday morning. By the Sunday evening they had gone, never to return, although the South Australians tried to lure them back at the end of the tour. Bligh's team could not play on the morning of their departure as they had in Colombo, because the Sabbath had to be observed. No time for free visits to the theatre, such as previous English teams in Adelaide had enjoyed. No time for a drive into the Mount Lofty Ranges, which give the Adelaide Oval much of its unique charm. No time for the nascent vineyards of the German-settled hinterland, and a sampling.

The 1882/83 team left on the SS *Kaiser-i-Hind* for Melbourne, where the prestigious cricket club was waiting for them. Bligh had not been able to play in Adelaide, but he was able to remove temporarily the sling on his right arm before the *Kaiser* docked at Williamstown pier, with a view to shaking hands with his hosts, drinking toasts, and meeting many men – and women.

On the evening of their arrival a large dinner was held in the honour of Bligh and his team by the Melbourne Cricket Club in their pavilion. Anyone who was anyone was present except for the Governor of Victoria, and he was only prevented by a death in his family. The team had been received at the pier by Sir William Clarke, among others, and a special train laid on to take them to Spencer Street station: easily arranged, as Bligh's hosts were the colony's Establishment. From the station they had been driven to the Oriental Club, and along the way the cricketers must have been impressed by the standard of living which had been attained in less than a century of Melbourne's existence. To the money which the free settlers of Victoria had brought with them to invest had been added the bounty from the gold-rush booms of the interior. From the station itself to the civic buildings and seats of government, their neo-classical exteriors radiated self-assurance. In the 1880s Melbourne bore many a similarity with New York; only there the comparison stayed, for New York continued to welcome the energies of fresh immigrants, while Melbourne preferred to remain starched, even bleached, until after the Second World War.

Before the evening dinner the English team had been given a champagne reception, and Bligh had met two sons of Charles Dickens; the novelist himself was a frequent visitor to Cobham Hall. The first English cricket team to Australia had, of course, only been assembled as an alternative attraction after the illustrious author had turned down an offer by the restaurateurs Spiers and Pond to make a reading tour of Australia. In the evening the cricketers were driven to the Melbourne Cricket Ground (MCG) for the dinner starting at half past nine. Between two and three hundred 'of the most influential men in Melbourne' were invited to, in the words of one newspaper, 'a magnificent supper', filling two rooms in the pavilion.

This made an intimidating start for what was in some ways the most important role of the English cricket captain: his speeches, more than anything else, presented the public face of English cricket and set the tone for the tour. In the pre-television age the newspapers had even more influence on popular opinion than now, and they were represented at this dinner. Bligh had been able to have a couple of oratorical nets in Colombo and Adelaide, but this was his first major speaking engagement. At the age of 23, in a new country, and as the key figure in this undertaking, all the self-confidence bred by Eton and Cambridge was needed to overcome his natural diffidence. Intimidating on a wall of the pavilion at the MCG was a painting of Lord Harris, but he had been a good deal older. One advantage Bligh had, though, was that apart from Harris, his predecessors had not set the highest standard of rhetoric. W.G. Grace had been abrupt, if not graceless, and made virtually the same speech on every occasion. Jim Lillywhite, the son of a brick-maker, had educated himself admirably, but he was no Cicero and could not help making the point that his players were better behaved than Grace's: 'I would like to propose the health of the XXII, between whom and myself not one difference has arisen throughout the match' Lillywhite had said in Adelaide after a game against South Australia in 1876/77. 'That is more than can be said for some of the matches played in Australia during my last visit.' Long before the end of Bligh's tour, the captain was confiding to his diary that the speech-making took a lot out of him.

Clarke proposed toasts to the Queen and the absent Governor. As vice-president of the Victoria Cricket Association, Mr F.G. Smith then gave a long and portentous speech, at the end of which he invited the audience to give the Hon Ivo Bligh a most hearty and cordial reception. Loud cheering made a promising start. So did some self-deprecation too: Bligh found it very difficult to express how grateful he and his team were for the welcome they had received. They had had a spot of bad luck: he himself had cut his hand and George Vernon had hurt his leg in Colombo. The bad luck, however, could have been worse: the ship they had come out on (the *Peshawur*) had been involved in a collision, but the ship which they had originally booked (the *Austral*) had sunk in Sydney Harbour. Turning his attention to the Australian team which had toured England, and which had yet to return to Australia, Bligh said that he had come to beard the lion in his den. This prompted cheers and laughter, and some witty heckler corrected him by shouting 'the kangaroo'. In a speech at Adelaide Bligh had mentioned 'the ashes', but nobody knew what he was talking about: the news of Australia's victory at the Oval had arrived, but nothing of the idea conceived by Reginald Brooks. During his landmark speech in Melbourne Bligh is not recorded as having mentioned any ashes. They were soon to come alight.

*   *   *

On their second evening in Melbourne, Wednesday 15 November 1882, Bligh went to Sunbury for the first time, where he met

Florence Morphy. The evidence for this date comes from the obituary of Florence, then the Dowager Countess of Darnley, in what had been the couple's local newspaper, the *Gravesend Reporter*, in 1944. This newspaper must have had regular access to both her and her late husband.

> The romantic story of her wedding, which was supposed to have originated by the meeting of her future husband (the late Earl) on the cricket ground at Melbourne, is known the world over. Unfortunately, it lacked the merit of being strictly true. Actually she was introduced to Lord Darnley (then the Hon. Ivo Bligh) at a dinner at the residence of Sir William and Lady Clarke the night after his arrival from England. Lord Darnley had his arm in a sling – he had hurt it during a tug of war on the boat and was thus unable to play in the opening match. Subsequently at Melbourne, he cut his finger while fielding the ball and his bride-to-be bound it up for him in the pavilion.

Confirmation, of a sort, comes from more contemporary sources. When Bligh wrote home to his father on 3 January 1883, he mentioned that he had gone to Sunbury and met Miss Morphy there four times. We know Bligh and his fellow amateurs were at Rupertswood on New Year's Eve, 1882; from 19 December (Bligh, in his eagerness, arrived two days earlier) until Boxing Day; and, before then, from 25 to 27 November. Given they arrived in Melbourne on 14 November, and had to play in Bendigo and Castlemaine before 25 November, Bligh did not have much time to make the first of his four visits to Rupertswood except at the outset. It is only natural too that he should have gone there at the first opportunity. 'Come over and have dinner with us' we can hear William or Janet Clarke saying, perhaps adding: 'We've got someone you might like to meet.'

Bligh's diary notes that his team had two hard days of practice at the MCG on Wednesday and Thursday, 15 and 16 November, ahead of the match against Victoria. This gives the lie to the assumption that cricketers of this era did not practise, though not all England XIs were as assiduous as Bligh's. The side that lost the inaugural Test turned up in Melbourne the night before the game, to face a well-drilled Australian side that had been practising for five days. Of the practice Bligh wrote in his diary: 'very sorely needed. Still hand laid up, will be for a fortnight. MCC ground very well appointed, splendid wicket.'

The captain was being reserved when he did not mention what he did in the evening, for usually he recorded the main social events, especially if a dance was involved. But he would not have been letting his side down if he had popped over to Sunbury of an evening, a 33-kilometre journey from Melbourne which could be made in half-an-hour if a special train were laid on to Rupertswood.

*   *   *

Outside Spanish America, few more ambitious attempts than Rupertswood have been made to recreate Europe in the southern hemisphere. Sir William Clarke's father, the emigrant from Somerset who was known as 'Big Clarke', had bought 31,000 acres in 1850, but construction of the mansion was not commenced until after his death. Then it was Master Rupert, the Clarkes' son who became the second Baronet, who laid the foundation stone in 1874 in front of his parents and named the place after himself.

Rupertswood is a two-storey building in Italianate style on a slight rise overlooking Jackson's Creek. In their prime, the fifty rooms would have constituted a dazzling display of marble fireplaces imported from Italy, along with the craftsmen to install them; of marble statues; of cameos on the ceiling and roses in gold leaf; of chandeliers and stained glass windows; of excellent reproductions of Titian and Raphael. If this mansion was not quite fit for a king, it was where the Duke of York stayed in 1901 for the opening of Australia's first Federal Parliament, and he was to become King George V.

The gardens consisted of 99 acres tended by more than 40 gardeners; so the historian of Rupertswood, Joy Munns, has established. The artificial lake was made by damming a creek, and built in the shape of Australia without Tasmania. To illuminate his

Europe-in-Australia, William Clarke installed his own gasometer, which turned kerosene into gas for lights for the rooms and stairs. The horses' stables were so fine that when the Clarke family had to sell Rupertswood in the 1920s, to a Roman Catholic teaching order called the Salesians, they were turned into classrooms.

Even when the main buildings were finished in 1876, William and Janet were not satisfied. They decided they needed a ballroom – and it is just as well for cricket that they did. The new ballroom became the talk of the colony, according to Ms Munns, and it must have dazzled an impressionable 23-year-old Englishman in particular. It had mirrors on the walls, five chandeliers, a marble fireplace and a bandstand. It was partly to avoid the noise and dust of construction that the Clarkes toured England in 1881/82; and happily, so far as Cupid was concerned, the ballroom was ready on their return.

England cricket captains on tours of Australia have always needed some escape, especially when their team has been losing. They have found this escape in different ways, either by creating their own space or retreating into a literal one. Wally Hammond, after losing the First Test of 1946/47 at Brisbane, climbed into a car and drove to Sydney without a word to his passengers, who included Len Hutton; and when Hutton lost the First Test of 1954/55 at Brisbane, he climbed into a car and drove to Sydney without a word to his passengers. Some captains, like M.J.K. Smith in 1964/65 or Nasser Hussain in 2002/03, have had their families with them to help them find solace. Bachelors have often grinned, and drunk, then drunk some more, and thereby borne the stress.

In this alien land Bligh naturally clung to those who wanted to befriend him, and at Rupertswood he surely found a most agreeable retreat. He had known the Clarkes now for over two months, seeing them almost daily, knowing they were 'of the right sort'. Their mansion offered an ease and spaciousness – a settled softness, ahead of the rest of Australia – which were not only attractive in their own right but fondly reminded him of Cobham Hall. It was a rural retreat too, and Bligh was always a man of the countryside in preference to the city. Whenever he stepped off the train at

Rupertswood's own station, and walked through the grounds past the lake up to the mansion, he must have felt some peace of mind, if it was not disturbed by matters of the heart. He would have been shown to a guest room, with its own marble wash-stand, overlooking the garden; he would have been entertained to dinner in a dining-room which could seat thirty people; he would have relaxed afterwards over port and cigars in the Smokers Room, talking with Sir William about the cricket or other matters; and whiled away the rest of his evening in the Billiard Room or Ballroom.

When he first visited Rupertswood, we know that Bligh had his right arm still in a sling: an injury which did not prevent him dancing, only batting. Before his arrival, Lady Janet Clarke had had a little time to tell her companion all about Ivo. Having arrived in Melbourne on the *Peshawur* (while Bligh and his men spent the weekend playing in Adelaide), Janet had a couple of days' start in which to brief Florence. She would have been able to tell her what Bligh looked like, might even have been able to show Florence a sketch of him that she had made during the voyage. She would have been able to tell Florence how tall he was, how elegant, and how gentle a gentleman he was. She would not have been able to inform Florence exactly about his prospects, but perhaps gave some details of his background of Cobham Hall, Eton and Cambridge. And in the refined atmosphere of Rupertswood, where ladies were trained to behave with the same decorum as in *Picnic at Hanging Rock*, the whispered plans would have bloomed like orchids.

Even though his diary makes no mention of his first meeting with Florence, we know that Bligh's writing routine was disturbed at exactly the time of his introduction to her. He normally made entries in his diary with the day of the week and the date alongside: 'Saturday Nov 11th', for example, was the second day of their Adelaide match. Even on the October day when he cut his hand in the tug-of-war, he entered the day and date as 'Wednesday 25', albeit a fortnight or so after the event. But his entry for the day when he must have first met Florence is simply headed 'Wednesday and Thursday' without any date at all.

The last entry in Bligh's diary covers the Castlemaine match on

24 and 25 November, which takes us up to page 25. This is not the end of this slim volume, however, for three more pages follow. They are given over to a prose-poem which has no title but is devoted to Rupertswood, and Bligh's feelings about it, and the 'fair lady' who presides over the place, Lady Janet Clarke. A photograph shows Janet with wider and fuller lips than the norm in Australia, with hair bunched up and dark eyes of some intensity. Bligh saw her chief characteristic as 'kind unselfishness', and her appearance does suggest she was kind and unselfish – provided, perhaps, she had her way.

As a late Victorian gentleman Bligh was reserved in prose, let alone speech, but he expressed his sentiments in this poem at the back of his diary. It would seem to have been composed on the voyage home from his tour of Australia around the month of May 1883, and it conveys the high emotions which Bligh experienced at Rupertswood during the tour. Without the numerous crossings-out and revisions it reads:

> Once more alas a weary traveller I sit
> And strive to keep a promise made to you long since
> That I a few short lines would write for that small book
> Which in its compass holds so many gems of thought.

This would seem to refer to 'a pocket-book', which a lady of this period such as Janet was required to keep to record her more intelligent thoughts and observations. The poem goes on:

> How hard it seems ay, cruel hard that word goodbye
> Is ever on our lips to soil the memory
> Of all our joyous days; tis sad but all too true.
> This world's a world of partings. While I speed my way
> This thought doth e'er beset me. Since these last few months
> I've found another home and friends as kind and loved
> As e'er I had before upon old England's shores.
>
> I'm going home and yet the while I'm leaving home –
> And while these weary days their dreary length do drag

I sit and solitary my lingering thoughts
Slowly take them back through all the pleasant days
I've passed since first we met upon old Father Thames.

What pleasant times there were upon that good old ship
What games we played, what cosy teas at four o'clock
You did dispense so kindly to us thirsty ones.
How did the Smiler laugh – Tylie smile, how
Anon the clarion note of Nat did pierce the air.

After eight more lines, more revised than most, in which he recalls
the collision and 'how near did the Peshawur a traitor prove and
yield us to those hungry waves', Bligh concludes:

And then at last the goal was reached: a few short months
Yes all too short we've spent on dear Australian shores.
Shall we e'er play again such well and hard-fought fights
At cricket as we then did play. No not again I think
Nor should we ever meet with such gracious encouragement
As came from that gay corner, where our roseate bands
Were worn by your fair ladies. And then best of all
What many days and nights there were at Rupertswood.
Ah dear old Rupertswood and you its denizens
Among the first and dearest, you'll e'er hold a place
Of all my memories. How I shall hail the day
When once again I shall see your walls, how every look
On you recalls some kindness ministered to me
By your possessors. In your ground and spacious hall
With what light hearts and glad we danced the whole night
    through.
And how did some of us within your precincts
Our willing homage yield to charmers bright and fair.
Yes to those short months will some of us look back
Through all our lives as having been the origin
Of our best happiness. God grant it may be so
And now all this is past there's but the one thought that
Remains to cheer me.

Tis not I hope goodbye I say but au revoir
Were it to be goodbye that hopeless word

I could not say it for it would such sadness bring
To me already sad enough. May every happiness
Attend you in this life fair lady is the wish
And that most heartfelt too of one who has through all
This time admired much that kind unselfishness
That graces so your character and gained for you
A multitude of earth's best blessing friends
And I shall always think myself most fortunate
If I may find a place among that company.

It is doubtful whether any of the 28 subsequent captains who led
England Test tours of Australia was so romantic, and love-sick, and
old-fashioned chivalrous, as the Honourable Ivo Bligh. Plenty of
England captains have fallen for Australian women. He was probably the only one who did the honourable thing and married one of
the many 'charmers bright and fair' with whom he 'danced the
whole night through'. No wonder Bligh did not score many runs in
Australia. His eye was not always on the right kind of ball.

*   *   *

From the time they arrived in Melbourne, Bligh's team had six
weeks in which to prepare for the prosaic purpose of their tour: the
first of three 'international matches' against the Australian XI,
starting in Melbourne on 30 December. It sounds a long time for
preparation, but of the games they had to play in the next six weeks,
all of them were up-country and against odds, except for two first-
class matches. Of these two matches, one was to begin immediately,
against Victoria, on 17 November; the second was against New
South Wales in Sydney, starting on 1 December. Bligh recognised
the consequence of this fixture scheduling. In the lead-up to the First
Test England did not have enough hard cricket, he wrote in
Lillywhite's, and their batsmen in particular did not fully adjust to
high-class bowling in the novel conditions.

No less then than now, the opening game of every England tour
of Australia was carefully scanned for signs of weakness in the
visitors. Moreover, there was an extra pressure which modern

touring teams do not have. The financial success of Bligh's tour depended on the international matches being interestingly competitive and therefore attracting the crowds: no Board of Control was underwriting the costs if the tour failed as a commercial venture. Bligh felt a responsibility to his hosts at the Melbourne Cricket Club, as much as to his own players, to preside over a successful tour.

An excellent tactic in the opening game against Victoria set the tone for Bligh's tour: they would play to their strengths and make the most of what they had. William Cooper was Victoria's main bowler in the absence of the Test players, who were to return home at last from their tour of England, North America and New Zealand on the second day of this match. Cooper is said to have taken up leg-spin at the age of 27 (he was now 33), and had become so accomplished he had played in the 1881/82 Test in Melbourne against Alfred Shaw's all-professional England side, taking nine wickets for 200 runs. As novelty was even more of an asset for a spinner in the days before film and slow-motion replays, Cooper's flight was especially troublesome for batsmen who had not seen him.

Bates, however, had seen him on the 1881/82 tour, so when Bligh's team lost an early wicket – George Studd bowled off his legs by Cooper for 1 – Bates was promoted from the lower order, where he had batted at Adelaide and Colombo, to number three. Bates used his feet, played a driving game and seized the upper hand. 'Runs came at a great pace, the Yorkshireman punishing all very severely' wrote the correspondent for the *Sporting Life*, and this correspondent had some insight into proceedings as he was an anonymous member of Bligh's team, his byline being 'One of Them'. In his diary Bligh amplified: 'W.H. Cooper deceived one or two a bit at first. He certainly has an astonishing break on a fast wicket but is so high in the air that almost anything can be done with him. Bates cracked him properly, put in early to show us how he ought to be played.'

Victoria's leg-spinner took five wickets with his leg-breaks – 'corkscrews' was another term – but England, as they were called, finished with 273; the equivalent today would be a hundred more, if not a total of 400. Saturday brought a crowd of 12,000, double the first day's attendance, and they saw a dominating performance by

England's bowlers, even though they were much of a muchness in pace – all slow to medium – in the continued absence of Morley. The only variety they had was not an overarm bowler at all, but the lobs of the Surrey amateur Walter Read. He is a likely candidate to have been 'One of Them', Steel another. Read needed the money for a start, for although he was officially an amateur he found it difficult to make ends meet, until he was given the post of Surrey assistant secretary – the customary designation in those times for an amateur paid to play cricket. Aged 27 on this tour, he had tried school teaching but did not have the temperament for coping diligently with the young. In the Oval Test of 1884, he was so annoyed when Lord Harris sent him in at number ten that he hit the Australian bowlers for 117 in just over two hours. Read's hundred remains the highest Test innings by an England number ten.

Read wrote a book at the end of his playing days, so he had the writing ability to have been the anonymous correspondent. The reports themselves also contain the odd hint that he was 'One of Them'. When England bowled, a subjective element appears in the match report when Read takes the ball. 'Though several changes of bowling were tried, the score had been carried to 40 when the England captain deputed Read to bowl underhand slows. These were evidently adverse to the taste of the Colonial cricketing public, although after having been no-balled, the Surrey amateur clean bowled Turner, who had scored 25 by good cricket.' In other words, Read was booed for attempting something so cissy and outdated as under-armers, but the report enables him to save face. Even Bligh described them in *Lillywhite's* as 'not very formidable lobs'.

Victoria were dismissed for 104, and were compelled to follow on as they were more than 80 behind. Through more poor batting the colony had lost seven more wickets for 121 by the close, and seemed set for an innings defeat on the Monday, even though rain delayed the resumption until 2.30 p.m. Then England were held up by a new player called William Bruce, who had been selected for his left-arm bowling. He had only taken one wicket, but he now showed distinct promise with the bat at number eight and made a hard-hit 40, which was just enough to make England bat again. Bruce was not yet twenty, and went on to become the first left-handed specialist batsman chosen by Australia for a tour of England, in 1886. (Bruce in old age fell on hard times and was found drowned near Melbourne.) Although England batted again, they did not have to score a run off the bat in order to complete a ten-wicket victory. Victoria's opening bowler Patrick McShane, quick left-arm, obliged by sending the first ball for four byes (he ended up in a mental asylum).

The second first-class match, against New South Wales (NSW), followed the same lines for the same reasons. England batted well on a good pitch and won convincingly, while the home side lacked quality in the absence of their Test players, who had returned to Australia but gone off to play an exhibition game in Adelaide. Like Victoria, New South Wales had one effective bowler – in this case Edwin Evans – and, after a first-innings collapse, one batsman who made a decent score in their second innings. Bligh observed at the tour's end that the number of cricketers in Australia of first-class standard was surprisingly small: outside the Test team, he reckoned there were no more than 20 players who would have been worth a place in an English county team. The Australian Test players of the 1880s – half-a-dozen in Sydney, half-a-dozen in Melbourne – had their centres of excellence, their miniature academies. At the Sydney and Melbourne cricket grounds they could bat and bowl against each other on good practice pitches, talk about the game among themselves, and analyse techniques empirically, for no coaching books had yet been written. Thus the elite raised their standards; but the rest could make little progress at club practices once or twice a week after work.

Evans was not only seen as the outstanding cricketer in the New South Wales side, he was seen by many as the outstanding cricketer in Australia for some years – without ever proving the point. It seems as though he was an elite athlete, the type a community throws up once in a generation. Cobbett wrote this profile for the *Sportsman*:

Standing well over 6ft, and considerably broader and thicker about the shoulder than most Australians are, Evans looks to the merest novice powerfully built. He is, too, a much better man than a casual glance would make him, and a keen judge can trace, in a certain indifferent carriage he has, indication of that combination of looseness of limb and great muscular power possessed by a few, but only a very few, really fine athletes. Either for sculling or throwing a cricket ball he is perfectly built, and when 'peeled' is much bigger than in his clothes, while every ounce of his weight (13st) is muscle or bone.

Evans was an all-rounder who batted right-hand, bowled off-breaks along with a quicker ball, and above all was a sensational fielder. In the public's eyes, Evans was the man, the cricketer of his time, ahead of Spofforth; but not, it seems, in Evans' own eyes. He had the body of an elite sportsman, but not the mind. The public saw his modesty, and loved him for it, but he was too modest for his own sporting good. The champion often has an obsession to make the most of his talents, and Spofforth had that cast of mind; Evans, not. Quiet and unassuming, Evans often did not turn up, or else found excuses; when Spofforth turned up, everybody knew. And so much did Spofforth resent the public esteem which Evans attracted that it was a source of motivation for The Demon.

On the first day, NSW were dismissed for 152; some of the batting was so artless against Steel's 'curly ones', his more highly tossed leg-breaks, that he took five wickets. On the second day, England scored at fine speed to take their total from 39 for one to 442 for eight, the highlight being the driving century by Leslie, who scored 93 runs in the morning session of one hour and a half. On the Monday England reached 461 – Evans bowled more than 80 four-ball overs to take six wickets – then dismissed NSW a second time for 165 to win by an innings and 144 runs. So disorganised were the state side in the absence of their Test men that they lost three wickets in the match to run-outs. Bligh concluded: 'Our opponents' list included the far-famed Evans, whose name has been so often impressed on us at home as that of the best all-round man in Australia, a title to which, at the present time, he is most certainly in no way entitled. Indeed, we rather question whether he would find a place now in their best eleven.'

Perhaps the most interesting feature of this match was the custom which then applied in Sydney and became a bone of contention when the Third Test was staged there. The custom was that the captain of each side at the start of a match, in addition to naming his XI, had also to decide which out of two prepared pitches he wanted his side to bat on. 'One of Them' described it as follows: 'The captains decided that the match should be played on two wickets, and that each eleven should play on the wicket selected by their captain, and not have the option of the choice of wickets.'

The custom seems to have arisen because, like most customs, it was dictated by circumstances. The outfield at the Sydney Cricket Ground (SCG) was ahead of its time, excellent for fielding, but the turf on the pitches was renowned for cutting up quickly. Having two pitches for a game meant that the totals, low enough, were not lower still. For the Fourth Test of the 1882/83 tour at Sydney, after the Third Test had ended there in a flurry of acrimony and low scores, the convention went further still by offering the captains no fewer than four pitches, which were duly accepted.

*   *   *

Bligh's team had ten up-country fixtures against odds, all of them two-day games except for that against XVIII of Ballarat, which was a three-dayer. The one against XVIII of Tamworth and District was pretty typical of a genre which no longer exists. Matches against odds disappeared from England fixture lists in Australia after the Second World War, while up-country games were terminated by World Series Cricket. Thereafter an international team could not waste time and money 'spreading the gospel' but had to keep earning major dollars.

In the 1880s these up-country games were made to pay their way. When the news reached Tamworth that Bligh's team were due to visit Australia, a local committee telegraphed an offer to Major Wardill, secretary of the Melbourne Cricket Club, offering to stage a two-day game against the tourists in return for a payment to the MCC of £200. Wardill asked for a deposit of £100, which was paid by the Tamworth committee who set about covering their costs. They began by recouping £125 by selling vending rights on the ground to licensed victuallers; tickets would offset the remaining £75. (On one early English tour of Australia, a publican who had bought the rights to stage a match tried to charge the players an entrance fee.) But a difficulty was that the normal cricket ground in Tamworth could not be legally fenced in to charge an entrance fee. The committee therefore decided to stage the big game at the racecourse.

It was fortunate no fast bowlers played. The area of the racecourse in front of the stand was mown; and coconut fibre matting was laid over 22 yards to form the pitch. At 4 p.m. on the afternoon before the game the English cricketers had arrived by train from Newcastle, when Tamworth station was 'densely packed', as all the local bigwigs had to meet them and get their name in the newspapers. At the stations on their journey the players had been welcomed by large crowds, who had been cheerfully polite in the main (the odd larrikin seems to have had a go). It is doubtful whether Bligh was in his element. Up-country towns had overwhelmingly male populations – a gender imbalance which was to apply in Australia until the middle of the twentieth century. Most of the professionals, and some amateurs, were not averse to talking and drinking in the bar but the captain would no doubt have preferred the company of ladies and, if possible, some dancing.

The value of these games for the tourists, in terms of practice, was minimal. The local club players had no chance of acquiring the necessary skills: the only worthy opponents England came across were men who had played in either Sydney or Melbourne before going up country. A fellow called Smith who had played state cricket scored 41; when Bligh's team played XVIII of Southern Tasmania they were bowled out for 110 by Tom Kendall, a slow left-armer who had been Australia's leading wicket-taker in the first of all Tests at Melbourne in 1877. But in general these enthusiastic clubbies were either clean-bowled for nought or stumped for a few more. We can imagine them walking out to bat in all manner of attire, wiping their hands on their trousers, spurning gloves even if they had any, and winding up to show the Poms a thing or two – before an accurate off-break from Bates or Barnes or Steel knocked over their stumps.

The unserious nature of this cricket did, however, allow for some serious sightseeing and socialising. In the Ballarat area the players were taken down gold mines in the morning before play; they sensibly decided to field first to re-adjust their eyes to the light of day. On the following tour in 1884/85 some of the English players were given shares in gold mines as rewards for their performances in two of the up-country games. They did not keep them, but made a fine profit when they auctioned off these shares.

A typical diary entry is for Tuesday 21 November, when Bligh notes that he attended Mrs John Blackwood's dance in Melbourne, while the other players set off for Sandhurst.

> I followed next morning very tired with Cobbett. Won the toss, made 100. We very bad start 4 wickets for 6. Wicket rather slow and number of fieldsmen round the wicket rather puzzling. Leslie saved us again with a well hit 48 not out. He is evidently quite got back to his best form. Morley still not playing . . . Hotel very fair, self in bed all Monday quite knocked up. Some of the team down gold mines. Get some good specimens. Most of team to Castlemaine Thursday evening. Self off to Sunbury Friday morning. Met Clarke going to Melbourne to Hanburys dance – to which three of team actually went in middle of match.

Bligh does not name and shame these players who bunked off during the game in Castlemaine, perhaps because he thinks he should not have left his team to visit Sunbury.

Castlemaine was renowned for having a lively pitch, if that is not too strong a term for the surface on which the match was played. On the 1873/74 tour led by W.G. Grace, his brother Fred had opened the batting there and been hit on the head by the first ball of the game. The Champion's fast bowler, Martin McIntyre of Nottinghamshire, managed the figures of twenty-one wickets for 36 runs against XXII of Castlemaine on that occasion. In 1882/83 Castlemaine's XXII stumbled to 22 for eight by the time stumps were drawn, even though Bligh's team had no fast bowler.

At Tamworth, Bligh objected to the locals playing XXII men, having found that it was hard work scoring runs when there were so many fielders clogging up the ground. After Tamworth lowered their numbers to XVIII, Bligh won the toss and decided to bat, and his opening batsmen went out to the middle, in front of a large and happy crowd, as special trains had brought in people from all over the district for this great day. And it promptly started to rain; and it rained all afternoon, and it rained the next day too, and not a single ball was bowled. The groundsman or curator, left in charge of the tourists' kit, sold some of it to a local pawnbroker before the hosts retrieved it. All that could be done was give the English cricketers a banquet at the Caledonian Hotel and send them on their way by train to Sydney. Once there seven of the amateurs went off to Moss Vale for some 'kangarooing and shooting'. Bligh went off alone, not to Melbourne initially, but to the SCG for some hard practice ahead of the First Test. He had so far played exactly one innings in Australia, when he opened the batting against XVIII of Newcastle and scored 22 before being stumped. After his practice at the SCG, the *Sydney Morning Herald* reported that the England captain 'appears to be rapidly getting into form'. His right hand was no longer aching, even if his heart was.

Following his initial visit to Rupertswood, Bligh returned there with the amateurs of his party on Saturday 25 November, arriving at ten o'clock in the evening after the game at Castlemaine. They remained there on the Sunday, went hare-shooting on the Monday, and returned to Melbourne by an early evening train. Bligh visited Rupertswood again, by himself, on Sunday 17 December, to be joined there by the amateurs two days later, where they remained until Christmas. And on Christmas Eve Bligh's men played a game of cricket on the paddock at Rupertswood, which culminated in the creation of the game's greatest prize.

5
The Substance

As Christmas Eve 1882 was a Sunday, it began with morning church. The Clarke family and their house-guests – including the Honourable Ivo Bligh, Edward Tylecote, Charles Leslie, George Vernon, Walter Read, Allan Steel and the Studd brothers, Charles and George – walked from Rupertswood to St Mary's Church of England in Sunbury. It is a solid, stone-built church, broad enough to have both feet on the ground, rather than tall and aspiring to flights of fancy. Here England's cricket captain was to be married in little more than a year.

After the service the Clarke party walked back to Rupertswood. A group photograph taken on the afternoon of this same day shows the gentlemen in dark jackets and top hats, the ladies in voluminous white dresses and bonnets. If the milieu was not exactly that of the girls' boarding school in *Picnic at Hanging Rock*, it would have been similar to the one created by Patrick White in *Voss*: the velvety atmosphere of the gracious family home in Sydney at this same period, where, as White recounted in one whole paragraph, 'Laura breathed.' The wealth of this new country – new to its European inhabitants – was channelled into the well-being and comfort of this elite.

On the way back to Rupertswood let us imagine the captain of the English cricket team catching up with Miss Florence Morphy, tipping his top hat to her and bidding her good morning. On the way to St Mary's she, as governess to the Clarke children, might have been too busy keeping an eye on Miss Blanche or Miss Ethel and

ensuring their petticoats were in order, or else talking with Lady
Janet about the social arrangements for later in the day. In the
afternoon a game of cricket was going to be played in the paddock.
On the morrow a dance, the favourite entertainment of England's
cricket captain, was to be held after the Christmas Day dinner – a
dance in which all the English amateurs, being single, would need
partners. In contemplating these possibilities Miss Morphy perhaps,
unlike Laura, held her breath.

As the eight English amateurs were so much better at cricket than
everybody else, it was decided they should form one team on their
own in the impromptu game. The home side was to consist of the
full eleven players – and of anybody else who wanted to play. After
luncheon the house-party walked down from the mansion to the
paddock, where trees offered copious shade and the slope a fine view
of proceedings. Stumps and bails had been borrowed from the
Sunbury cricket club, the pitch in the paddock well prepared.

Exactly what those proceedings were, we shall never know.
Cobbett was not a house-guest of the Clarkes, and no other reporter
was present. Not that this game of cricket needed to be recorded. It
was merely a spot of fun and exercise, nothing to desecrate the
afternoon of the Sabbath. When the Englishmen batted, they
delighted the watching ladies and men by their hits for four and six.
One of the workers on the Rupertswood estate, Pat Lyons, a
dairyman, played in the game against the Englishmen and recalled
in his bearded dotage how he had often collected the ball from
beyond the paddock near to the railway line.

After the game a now faded group photograph was taken of the
several dozen ladies and gentlemen, sitting on a grassy slope, all of
them dressed as elaborately in the heat as their descendants of today
would be skimpily clad. And a presentation was made. It was one of
the many happy ideas of Lady Janet Clarke, or perhaps of her
companion, Miss Morphy. Janet and her husband had been in
England when Australia had won the international cricket match at
the Oval and 'the ashes of English cricket' had been conceived by the
Sporting Times. The joke by now had reached the ears of Australia's
public. Four weeks before, on the evening of Monday 27 November

1882, a banquet had been held in Melbourne in honour of Billy Murdoch and his team who had returned from their victorious tour of England and North America. Sir William and Lady Janet were regrettably absent: they had to attend another banquet in Melbourne the same evening (to inaugurate the Clarke buildings which Sir William and his brother Joseph had endowed at Trinity Hall). The English cricketers, however, had attended the dinner in honour of Murdoch's men, where the Australian captain in his speech had revived the jest conceived by Reginald Brooks. Murdoch declared:

> Our boys fairly won the ashes and we confidently rely on them to retain possession, at least for the present. When, as we hope we have shown our visitors that they cannot recover the ashes, we can then place the sacred dust in a suitable urn in our Public Library, as a curiosity to be shown to visitors with respect and esteem as the result of the Australian prowess in the cricket field.

Bligh, as his letters reveal, did not hold his Australian counterpart in the very highest esteem. As he had read Trollope on the voyage out to Melbourne, the thought might have occurred to Bligh during this banquet that Murdoch was 'blowing', or not speaking with due modesty. In any event, Murdoch's speech was retold in the newspapers and must have reached Rupertswood – where the Australian captain was a frequent visitor himself – and the ears of the Clarkes. The ashes of English cricket: 'Our boys fairly won the ashes' Murdoch had said. Anybody in Australia who had an interest in cricket, and did not live way out in the bush, now knew about them.

So it was, at the end of this social match, that Lady Janet Clarke organised a presentation to the Honourable Ivo Bligh. It was the first of several gifts to be exchanged between the English cricketers and Australia's 'first family' over the period of Christmas and New Year. The amateurs were to present the Clarkes with a handsome silver salver with all eight of their names engraved upon it. The Clarkes – Janet, that is – were to present the cricketers with mementoes in precious metal of their voyage to Australia on the *Peshawur*.

For the moment, on Christmas Eve, the Clarkes presented to Bligh an urn containing some ashes as a memento of the game on the paddock that afternoon. One account says the original urn was made of gold; another of pottery. Many years later, in 1930, the Dowager Lady Darnley – as Florence had by then become – addressed the Australian cricketers led by Bill Woodfull on their tour of England. The occasion was a luncheon given in their honour by the International Sportsmen's Club at Grosvenor House in London. The Ashes themselves were present, on a table opposite the Dowager, who proceeded to tell the story of the urn. She stated that 'Lady Clarke, wife of Sir W.J. Clarke, who entertained the English so lavishly, found a little wooden urn, burnt a bail, (and) put the ashes in the urn.' Whatever its original substance, however, this urn was soon to be replaced by the terracotta urn which survives today.

As for the composition of these original ashes, there are almost as many accounts as for the urn. As the Dowager in 1930, Florence's testimony to the Australian touring team was that the ashes were those of a bail which Janet had burned – before placing them in the little wooden urn.

On the other hand, the dairyman Pat Lyons in his old age told Sir William's grandson, the Hon Michael Clarke, that the ashes were the burnt remains of the leather cover of the cricket ball used in that social game on Christmas Eve. Michael Clarke told Ronald Willis that Lyons had said: 'They knocked the cover off the ball, and afterwards it was burnt and the ashes put in a vase or something and given to the English captain, who married Florrie Morphy from Sunbury the following year. He was a lord and he took those ashes to England.'

This grandson, Michael Clarke, also told Willis:

My father, Russell Clarke, and my uncle, Sir Frank Clarke, used to argue whether the bails or ball were burnt. Local tradition favoured the ball, but my uncle had doubts as to whether one could burn a cricket ball. They agreed that it was not the stumps – which were borrowed from the local cricket club; and they thought that the bails would also be borrowed.

I don't know for certain whether the Rupertswood ashes are The Ashes or not, but my father and uncle were convinced they were, and expressed scorn of other stories about their origin. I gathered that the cricket historians were reluctant to accept a version based upon a social game at Rupertswood, and preferred one based upon a Test match or other grand occasion. I well remember visiting the then Lord Darnley at Cobham in England when I was a schoolboy (about 1933). He showed my mother and I over the house and remarked that both his mother and the cricket Ashes came from Sunbury.

Ultimately it does not matter what the original urn was made of, or whether the ashes were those of a bail used in the game, or of the leather cover of the ball, or of anything else used in the game. We will never know in any event, because the original contents were considerably diluted after at least one accident at Cobham Hall, and may have entirely disappeared. This would explain the reluctance of the Marylebone Cricket Club to allow DNA analysis.

What mattered was that the Ashes, having been conceived in England, had now been made in Australia. They were no longer a joke. They were an idea turned into reality by Lady Janet Clarke. And it was in a spirit of fun – perhaps of flirtatious, coquettish fun if Miss Morphy helped Lady Janet in the enterprise – that the Ashes were brought into being and presented to the captain of the English touring team.

But whatever the spirit in which the Ashes urn was created, England and Australia now had a prize for which to compete at cricket most seriously. People, and especially young men, are always interested in a quest – and, better still, a quest which has a material object. As a result of Bligh's tour, and his relationship with his hosts at Rupertswood, the sport now had its equivalent of the Holy Grail.

* * *

Dawn at Rupertswood on Boxing Day, 1882, found the Bligh spirits less than blithe. Before the First Test starting on 30 December, they had to play a three-day match at Ballarat, beginning at noon on Boxing Day. The amateurs were up so early for the private train from Sunbury to Melbourne that they caught the 6.30 a.m. from Spencer Street station to Ballarat, taking with them any lingering effects from dining and dancing in the ballroom at Rupertswood.

It may seem harsh and exclusive to us today that Bligh's four professionals spent Christmas in Melbourne, not as house-guests at Rupertswood. Yet Barlow, Bates, Barnes and Morley might not have felt comfortable on the country house circuit, certainly not the latter two Nottinghamshire men; Barlow, who could play a role and sing in amateur dramatics, and Bates, who was renowned for his smart dressing, are more likely to have fitted in. The professionals had put up at the Oriental in Melbourne, where the whole team had stayed on their arrival in the colony, and for ten days before Christmas they had the freedom of the city for their diversions. If they did not wish to attend the intercolonial match between Victoria and New South Wales at the MCG, or practise there, the city offered plenty of music besides eating and drinking. It was Barlow's task, as senior professional, to lead the group to Ballarat; and he dutifully did so on Christmas Day when they took the train from Melbourne.

The amateurs arrived in Ballarat at 10.35 a.m. on Boxing Day, ready for the noon start at the Eastern Oval. Or, to be precise, seven of the amateurs turned up to join the professionals, while Vernon missed the train. Bligh's accounts here are inconsistent. In *Lillywhite's* he wrote: 'Christmas activities had the effect of causing the team to arrive in Ballarat one short, the delinquent turning up in the course of the afternoon, with the novel excuse that he had not been called that morning at the hotel in Melbourne.' Yet Vernon, as one of the eight amateurs, had surely spent the night at Rupertswood – unless he had slipped away to the city, having other fish to fry. Which is conceivable, given that he played five internationals for England as a rugby player.

Bligh put his foot down for once when the match organisers at Ballarat told him the home side was going to consist of twenty men: he insisted that eighteen were enough. His report of the game in *Lillywhite's* is a sufficient summary of this warm-up before the opening Test:

> The eighteen were about the best that we met in the Colonies, and gave us considerable trouble to dislodge from the wickets, during their innings of 226 and 171, Lawler and Lewis, both young cricketers, playing in really capital style. The second day found most

of the team in good form, and the hitting towards the end became fast and furious, Read (55), the captain (45), and Tylecote (40 not out), being the principal scorers. With 126 to win, and the wicket still unimpaired, a pretty certain win was lost from want of time, and possibly, as the three days were uncommonly hot ones, with the great match impending, this was as well for the team. The ground, which was well kept, played easily, but was rather slow considering the dry weather.

Bligh's team, amateurs and professionals, returned to Melbourne together by the evening train on 28 December. The next day the MCG was being used for the last day of the intercolonial match, which had enjoyed a prolonged break over Christmas. Thus the Australian players in the Victorian and New South Wales teams had a day of match-play on the eve of the First Test. Most of the English team attended the intercolonial match at some time during the day, followed by another official dinner not only for themselves at Clement's Café but also the New South Wales and Victoria teams.

At noon on 30 December, at the MCG, the first of the three internationals against Murdoch's Australians was to begin, the main business of Bligh's tour. The English captain had only eleven players to choose from, because his leading bowler Morley had not been able to play in Ballarat and was, if anything, even more unfit than on the day they had arrived in Adelaide. But the cricket was not alone in weighing upon Bligh's mind. On returning from Ballarat to Melbourne he had received a letter, an admonitory letter, from Lady Janet Clarke. It was, we may deduce, a reply to a letter which Bligh had written to Janet declaring his love for Florence. Has any England captain ever gone into an Ashes Test in a greater state of mental turmoil than the 23-year-old who, unfortified by age or cynicism, had fallen head over heels?

The letter from Lady Janet, dated 28 December 1882, read as follows:

My dear Mr Bligh,

I was certainly very much astonished when I read your letter, and if you think of the matter (as I am quite sure you would, from what

I know of your character) as the very greatest steps in your life, you will not think me foolish in saying that I pray to be guided aright in advising you. You know that Miss Morphy is a very great friend of mine. I admire her for her unselfish devotion to her duty as much as for her beauty, and therefore you will know that in saying what I may, I can only be activated by one motive – your own good. First, have you considered your Father, and Mother, they have never seen her, and when they hear that their son – in whom so many hopes are centred – is about to marry a young lady whose family though good is very poor and who has herself to work as a governess, they may not be pleased. Miss Morphy's father was a police magistrate, and died many years ago, since then her mother has had a hard struggle to bring up her family. She had some gentlemen to live with her first, and then, as one by one her three daughters married, the first a barrister, the second a gentleman in the government service, and the third the same, she was able to give this up. Unfortunately the eldest sister's husband turned out badly, and she died leaving six children, all babies nearly. Then Mrs Morphy had again to set to, and Florrie too. The former is in charge of an establishment to aid governesses coming to this colony, the latter teaches some children in Melbourne, so between them they support these six children – there are I think two brothers on stations [i.e. farms]. Now dear Mr Bligh think of all this. Miss Morphy will stay with me for six weeks, and I give you free leave to come up here _every_ day you are in Melbourne. Come by all means on Sunday if you wish after what I have said, but be advised by me in this, do _not_ ask Miss Morphy on Sunday. She is not engaged to anyone, and so be more sure that in her you have found the one woman whom God intended to be your helpmeet, and solace through life. If you are quite sure that you will mutually [indecipherable word] and raise one another's characters then no-one will more sincerely wish you all and every happiness. If, on the other hand, you have been much attracted by a pretty face, and bright brave girl, she knows nothing of the deeper feelings you think you have, and you need never remember having written to me on the subject, as the matter will thoroughly rest between us.

May I say that in any case it would be both wise and truer to write home by the outgoing mail. You will have three months, in which time you can have an answer, and you will have an opportunity even in the short visits you pay to Melbourne of seeing more of her. In such a case do not be too hurried, and think of it in the same spirit as you did of the Collision, remembering that in all things in this world we may not act on our feelings but our judgment. Please do not think I have spoken too seriously, it is as I feel. I need not tell you the great interest and friendships we feel for you, and in that light take my advice, and very best wishes for your happiness in every sense. As I shall probably not have an opportunity of speaking more than a passing word on Saturday [the first day of the First Test], will you write me a line to say if you will come up on Sunday, perhaps one of the others would join you. If all care to come they are welcome and believe always your sincere and true friend

Janet Clarke

'Do not ask Miss Morphy on Sunday'. Reading between the lines of Bligh's next letter home, he was far too infatuated to obey Lady Clarke's advice. He was consumed by a burning passion.

*   *   *

Since the first of all Test matches in 1877, if not before, the burghers of Melbourne have driven their vehicles – horse-drawn or petrol-fuelled – to Yarra Park, and parked under the trees, before entering the Melbourne Cricket Ground to see great matches. They have taken sunshades and refreshments along with their expectations of a good day's sport, and Saturday 30 December 1882 was no different. In the words of *Sporting Life*:

The weather was of the most delightful description. Great interest was taken in the match from the fact that it was the first occasion upon which the English Eleven had met the champions of Australia since their return from England. The handsome ground of the Melbourne Club certainly looked its best upon this occasion. The Pavilion, from verandah to roof, was closely packed. The large Grand Stand, capable of holding 2,000 spectators, was fully occupied, whilst the gay dresses of the ladies, who patronised in large numbers the reserve set apart for their especial benefit, added light and colour to the scene. The ring round the ground, which is seated to accommodate about 8,000 spectators, as well as having a sloping embankment which extends some 30 ft. back, was crowded with people, and every place of vantage was occupied from which a sight of the game could be obtained, the estimated number on the ground being about 16,000.

The toss was important, although not decisive. It was not only a question of having first use of the pitch before it was cut up, in a period when there were no heavy, mechanised rollers to repair the turf. It was a question of the weather too. If the pitch began dry, and the game lasted two or three days, with a Sunday in between, it was likely that rain would fall on it at some stage, and neither in England nor Australia at this period did covers exist. This time it was Murdoch who won the toss, as he had done more often than not in England the previous summer. No need for one last inspection of the pitch before he chose to bat first.

Even then, for all the advantage which Australia had gained, they still had to bat well to exploit it – and for the first half of the day, until Australia had reached 162 for five, they batted no more than competently. England stayed in the game, as Bligh made up for the lack of variety in his bowlers by changing them around and giving all of them a go – all except for his absent fast bowler, Morley, who had reported rheumatism in his knee in addition to the inexplicable chest complaint. Apart from the slow to medium pace of Charles Studd, Barnes, Steel, Barlow and Bates, Bligh gave a turn to two other bowlers. One of them, Walter Read, was ineffective with his lobs and expensive too, and soon withdrawn. Bligh however plucked a rabbit out of the hat when he gave Charles Leslie a turn. At Oxford he had seldom bowled but he was young, fit and willing to have a go, and he had tried five overs as the seventh bowler in Ballarat; and even a bit of inaccurate pace was going to break up the sameness of the rest of England's bowling. Bligh did not call on him in the first session, when Australia cautiously reached 46 for the loss of Hugh Massie, who was caught and bowled by Studd. But once the score had reached 70 for one in the afternoon session, Bligh gave Leslie the ball – and almost produced the first hat-trick for England.

Leslie was not so quick that Tylecote could not stand up to the stumps: 'Tyley' indeed stood up to all but the fastest bowlers, a good old-fashioned stumper, and was one of the first keepers in England to dispense with a long stop. Murdoch clearly did not think much of the new bowler, but he picked the wrong ball to hit and lost his off stump. Tom Horan came in and edged his first ball from Leslie to Barlow at slip. In two balls Australia had gone from 81 for one to 81 for three – at the hands of a bowler who took only eight wickets in his first-class career. Percy McDonnell kept out the hat-trick, but before Leslie's spell and puff came to an end, he had conjured a third wicket, although as it was a stumping down the leg side, perhaps more of the credit should go to Tylecote. A stumping off a wide half-volley down the leg side from a wild, occasional pace bowler: wicketkeeping does not come much better than that at any stage of cricket history. Some credit to Bligh too for his captaincy. 'Leslie got 3 of the best wickets for 31 runs!' Bligh informed his father in a letter home, using an exclamation mark, something he used with restraint, unlike his contemporary Queen Victoria. 'Murdoch, Bannerman and Horan – on these good wickets a wild bowler like that seems the best chance of getting wickets.'

At this point, when Australia were 162 for five, came George Bonnor. 'The Australian Giant', he was called, or else 'the Australian Hercules'. He was the tallest Test cricketer of the nineteenth century, 6ft 6in, and immensely strong but well-proportioned. W.G. Grace, or maybe his ghost, lyrically called him 'a fine specimen of physical beauty'. The Doctor's younger brother Fred had caught Bonnor in the 1880 Oval Test off such a steepling hit that the batsmen had turned to run a third. Bonnor's power and co-ordination were such that on a voyage to England he struck a bet that he could throw a cricket ball one hundred yards on landing without any warming up, and he more than made the distance.

It was a brave man who incurred Bonnor's wrath – and one who had done so was the Nottinghamshire secretary, Captain Holden, on the Australians' 1882 tour of England. From the first tour there had been a debate as to whether the Australians were amateurs or professionals, as they occupied a grey area in between. They were being paid to tour England, but they had jobs at home; they received broken-time payments in effect. Some counties called the tourists

'Mr' or 'Esq.' on their scorecards; others gave only their surnames as if they were professionals. Captain Holden was not in two minds: to him the Australians were professionals and to be treated as such. They could therefore buy their own lunch and queue for it in the refreshment tents with the rest of the public, while the amateurs were having their luncheon in the pavilion. Bonnor was so incensed that he had to be restrained. Holden imperiously took out a cigar and asked: 'Will some Englishman give me a light?' Bonnor gave an immediate insight into Australian identity at the time when he replied: 'I can tell you, sir, I am as much an Englishman as you or any gentlemen present; I can trace my family back for six generations and perhaps you cannot do more.'

As a batsman, or hitter, Bonnor was the Adam Gilchrist or Andrew Flintoff of his time; at number seven, he was the man who could take a game away in less than an hour. He had batted up the order in the 1882 Oval Test, at number three, when the fast bowler George Ulyett had been brought on to get Bonnor early and bowled him. Bligh's team had no fast bowler to trouble him, nobody of any pace after Leslie was spent. The game was in the balance as George Giffen was joined by Bonnor, who took it by the horns.

Bligh was well aware that it was 'game on'. Bonnor, he told *Lillywhite's*, 'soon began hitting in that truly terrific manner that has demoralised so many sides.' In knocking up 60 not out before the close of the first day Bonnor hit four sixes in our terms. But a hit over the boundary, or, as the Melbourne newspapers said, 'the chains', only counted five runs then; to count six it had to go out of the ground. Bonnor would have done this, off one of Read's lobs, had the ball not hit a tree – a hit 'into the pavilion reserve, which, had it not struck a pine tree, would have gone over the outer fence for 6.'

Under this assault England's fielding wilted, as most sides wilt to this day, and the captain was powerless to prevent it. 'The fielding of England was not at all up to the usual standard, several runs being thrown away, as well as chances missed in the field' noted *Sporting Life*. Before Bonnor came in, there had been only one catching chance of note, a 'hot' one offered by McDonnell to Read at mid-on; and one stumping chance offered by Giffen off Steel, when

Tylecote had slipped, suggesting that he wore no studs. After Bonnor came in, five chances were put down. First it was Bonnor dropped at long-on when Barlow got a hand to the ball; the second when Bonnor hit Steel to Read on the boundary, when the chance was 'badly missed'. The other three chances were all offered by Spofforth towards the end of Australia's innings: one to the keeper, a second to Barlow at slip, and 'the easiest of chances' off Studd to Steel at cover-point. But Spofforth made only 9 and Australia were 251 for seven when he came in, almost out of sight, given the rain to come.

'One of Them', the correspondent for *Sporting Life* who was an English player, did have two excuses to offer; if he was Read, he had plenty to explain away. 'It is only fair to say, however, that, although the wicket played exceedingly well, the out-fielding ground was decidedly rough. This may, with justice, plead a sufficient excuse for occasional misfielding . . .' True, as the mechanised heavy roller had not been invented, it was much harder to stop the ball on rough ground. For his second excuse, 'One of Them' advanced: 'The dark foliage of the trees which surround the Melbourne Cricket Ground is no doubt answerable for the missing of many a catch, for when the ball drops in a line with any of these trees it is most difficult to keep in view.' Bligh in *Lillywhite's* allowed himself to say: 'our ground fielding was, as usual, well on the spot, and G.B. Studd did some really splendid work.'

After play, Bligh and the amateurs repaired to Rupertswood. The next day, New Year's Eve, was a Sunday and therefore a rest day. It is unlikely Bligh had much rest: in going from the MCG to Rupertswood he was simply swapping one pressing matter for the next. In view of the letter he was write to his parents within four days, it would seem correct to surmise that Bligh proposed to Florence on New Year's Eve in spite of Lady Clarke's advice not to ask her. A dinner and a dance were held at Rupertswood to see in the New Year. What better setting could there have been for the two young lovers?

Something else of importance happened on Sunday 31 December 1882. Rain came. It had rained on Saturday night too. On Monday morning, New Year's Day, it rained again, according to Bligh, who took up the story in a letter to his father on 7 January 1883:

> When I got to the ground I felt convinced that the match was practically over. Our lot played up well the first innings but 2nd innings when the wicket had improved a bit went to pieces rather and in the end we were beaten (by) 9 wickets. I personally had a bad time of it as was only likely under the circumstances. I had only had 2 days practice on a fast ground and 2 innings both on slow grounds. I knew it was unlikely I should get runs especially with my hand still weak and I did not. First innings rather unlucky, pulled an off ball into the wicket, 2nd innings clean bowled with a long-hop by Spof. Palmer's bowling was very good, his breakback at times almost unplayable.

A crowd of 20,000 turned up on New Year's Day after England had finished off Australia's innings for 291 and stumbled to 7 for two wickets by lunch. The pitch had been given the roller but, being unmechanised, it may have been too light to have had significant impact. Bligh opened in England's first innings, then promoted Tylecote to open in the second and dropped himself to number five, to no avail. England's lunchtime position was worsened straight afterwards when Charles Studd was bowled 'by a tremendous breakback from Spofforth' (*Sporting Life*). Spofforth could have been expected to run amok on this damp pitch, as he had at the Oval, but he took only three more wickets, as well as having two slip catches dropped. Perhaps it was too easy for him after this breakback had reduced England to 8 for three wickets in their first innings; his demonic nature needed more of a challenge. But Spofforth went wicketless in the Second Test when Australia did need him. The explanation may lie in the fact that his elder (and only) brother Edward was ill. He was living in northern New South Wales at this time and known to be suffering from some mental or nervous condition. On 15 September 1883, Edward Spofforth died at the age of 35.

Barlow tried blocking his way out of trouble, Steel and Bates hitting. Bates hit Palmer for five before more rain fell, and on resumption another wicket did too. Later, Tylecote and George Studd found themselves at the same end, whereupon Blackham ran with the ball to the other end to remove the bails. True to character, Studd 'with considerable self-sacrifice stepped out from his crease, and allowed Tylecote to keep possession.' When Vernon came in as last man to join Barnes, England still needed 55 to save the follow-on, as the follow-on margin then was only 80 runs. The last pair managed 21, before Barnes was bowled by an off-break from Palmer which 'broke a foot' – or so Barnes said to 'One of Them'. England scored 177 in their first innings, 114 behind, and had to bat again, whether the Australians liked it or not. Barlow and Tylecote reached 11 without loss by the close of the second day.

If there was a grim inevitability about the final day, 16,000 Australians still wanted to see it. England did quite well to reach 164 for five in their second innings. No English batsman in either innings reached 40, although Tylecote showed good sense to top-score in both; indeed he and his Australian counterpart Jack Blackham, through the habit of watching the ball more closely perhaps than their team-mates, seem to have been their sides' best batsmen on bad pitches. Then, not for the last time in a Melbourne Test, England lost three wickets without adding a run and were all out for 169. Almost needless to say, the Australians thought there was nothing wrong with the pitch, after lunch on the second day at least, and everything with England's batting. 'Infelix' in the *Australasian* was as unsympathetic as any:

> The first two wickets of the Englishmen fell before lunch, and they had bad luck in having to bat when the wicket favoured the bowlers, but even after luncheon, when very little, if any, fault could be found with the wicket, the Britishers were altogether non-plussed by Palmer's superb bowling, and their friends were quite rueful and long-visaged when batsman after batsman fell before the beautiful break-backs of the South Melbourne crack . . . The credit of lowering the English wickets so rapidly and of gaining so brilliant a victory for Australia is due to the grand bowling of Palmer, Giffen, Garrett, and Spofforth, and especially Palmer, who during his career never bowled as well as he did in the first innings of this match, when he

came out with the splendid figures of seven wickets for 65, and when he bowled with a precision of pitch and variety of pace and break such as caused more than one of the Englishmen to say that they had never seen anything to surpass the bowling of the young South Melbournite.

Australia needed only 56 to win, and knocked the runs off after losing an early wicket. England bowled very tightly – the Australians needed the equivalent of 35.3 six-ball overs to score the runs – but the only wicket to fall was that of Massie, in almost freakish circumstances. Massie hit a skier off England's opening bowler Barnes, and the sun got into his eyes. Quickly improvising, Barnes screened his eyes with one hand, presumably his left, and caught the skier with the other. The pragmatic Bligh was all in favour, applauding 'a presence of mind – or, more strictly speaking, of hand – that did him credit.'

'Infelix' had not finished, however. He was to save his unkindest cut for one short last paragraph that speaks of an early sense of nationalism: 'The bowling of the Englishmen to my mind is much inferior to that of the Australians, and herein lies the superiority of our men.'

*   *   *

On the evening of this third day, after the match, Bligh did not have to give press interviews or make television appearances. It might have been less arduous if he had. He and the rest of his team had to attend a banquet – no chance of refusing as it was being given by Sir William Clarke – and he, as captain, had to give a speech, through gritted teeth. Using the vocabulary of England cricket captains to come, he used the phrase 'disappointing' to describe the result. The rest of Bligh's speech was summarised as follows in the press:

Some might be inclined to say he was a big duffer responding for a lot of big duffers. (Cries of 'No, no' and laughter.) The last time he made a speech in Melbourne he said the team came out with the hope of bearding the lion or kangaroo in his den: but he was afraid, looking at the result of the last match, that it must be confessed that the kangaroo had hopped a considerable distance in front. (Laughter.) But they did not despair. They hoped to have two other shots at the kangaroo, and their late defeat would only make them strain every nerve to turn the tide of victory. He referred to the warm feeling of friendship existing between the two teams, and bore testimony to the impartiality and to the spirit of fair play exhibited by the Australian public during the progress of the matches.

Next day England's captain had an even more pressing concern than the Test series on his mind. In his best handwriting, and in ink, Bligh wrote as follows:

Melbourne
Jan 3rd
    My dearest Father and Mother,
    You will see on reading this why I address the letter to you both, as it is perhaps the most important letter I shall ever write to you. Many thanks for your letters by the last mail which were written directly after you had read the accounts of the collision. I am so glad that you all did not realise the danger at first from the telegrams. Please thank all the others for their nice letters too. Now for the main subject of my letter. To go straight to the point at once I want your permission to marry an Australian young lady Miss Florence Morphy. I will tell you the whole story. To begin with you doubtless remember how much I have told of Mr and Mrs (now Sir W. and Lady) Clarke. Well we have seen a great deal of them out here and their country house Rupertswood. Sunbury has been quite a home to us. I have been there 4 times. I met this young lady both staying at the Clarkes (every time), she being one of Lady Clarke's greatest friends, and also in Melbourne and I am perfectly and most firmly convinced that she is the woman who would make my life a happy one. I do not mean to go into a description of her here but I will only say that as sure as I sit here she is a girl that all of you would love almost as soon as you saw her. A more truly lovable character I have never met in man or woman and whatever you think about the matter I must assure you most solemnly that this is no case of a young fellow being caught by a pretty face. I do not at all know what you will say to this. Whether you think me too young or whether you

can afford to let me marry but I must say this, that I would do anything rather than give her up. Supposing you cannot afford to set me up in business in England I would stay out here where one can get on on so much less and do any work I could get. I have had an idle time of it up till now and I'm ready if necessary to put my shoulder to the wheel. I have not told you yet that this young lady is very poor, her father who was a police magistrate having been dead many years and she and her mother have had hard work to support the orphan children of one of her sisters. That you would think no less of her for that I think I know you too well to have any such idea. For my own part I honour and respect her all the more for it. At the same time though poor she is in the best society in Melbourne and as I said before she is, which speaks volumes for her true worth, Lady Clarke's dearest friend, the friend of one of the kindest and truesthearted women that ever stepped this earth. I have spoken to Miss Morphy on the subject and unworthy as I am of it she returns my love – but I told her that I would not ask her to give me a certain answer till I had heard from you which the dear girl that she is entirely acquiesced in, and particularly told me to tell you the whole circumstances of the case before she wd [sic] answer me for certain. So true hearted is she that I believe were you not to give me your full consent she would forgo her love for me sooner than cause any one pain by her act. What my wish is to marry this girl and the sooner the better. I am willing to do anything in the world to bring about this object and my choice is <u>irrevocably</u> fixed. That this should have happened when I am so far from home so that you cannot even see the young lady is of course most unfortunate but it's a mischance that might happen to any one and I must ask you trust me up to this point that this young lady is everything that you could wish for as a daughter in law. Could you send me a telegram when you get this letter just to say you have received it and do telegraph also just that wished for affirmative to say that you give your permission. [indecipherable word] which I would like to do is to get the wedding over and come home as soon as possible but that can be soon arranged once the main point is settled. The Clarkes will see me through the matter out here I know. I don't think I told you that the young lady is I <u>believe</u> 2 years younger than me. Now I have finished the matter I think and I shall watch anxiously for your answer believing fully that you will do your best for your most devoted son
Ivo

Just been defeated by Australian XI. All the worst of luck. They had dry wicket Saturday – rain came Sunday, Monday morning and evening.

At least the First Test match had merited a postscript in the English captain's letter.

6

Cutting Up Rough

England had to wait a little more than a fortnight before the 'must-win' Second Test, which was also to be staged at the Melbourne Cricket Ground. They spent most of this time in Tasmania, which English touring teams through the ages have found therapeutic. The island is more reminiscent of rural England than of the Australian mainland.

Bligh's team had lost the First Test. But *The Times* in London reported that England, not Australia, had won by nine wickets. Bligh's father immediately sent a telegram of congratulations to his son. In his next letter home Ivo said responsibility for the mistake lay with a telegraph clerk, not with Cobbett, the sole English journalist on the tour; and the chance of human error was considerable in the repeater stations spread along the route from Melbourne to Adelaide to Alice Springs to Darwin, where the line went under the sea to Colombo.

As Bligh's team left Melbourne, the Australian press did not neglect the opportunity of rubbing in their country's victory: *plus ça change*, it might be commented. *Punch*, the Australian *Punch*, made merry with the following satire – including the odd punch below the belt – on 4 January, two days after England's nine-wicket defeat. This piece imagines an interview between the English captain and Mr Punch.

'Honourable, we are delighted to make your acquaintance,' we cried, rising, and shaking him warmly by the hand. 'You and your team appear to be a fine gentlemanly lot of young fellows, and you play an excellent game of cricket.'

The Hon Ivo fidgeted about this, and leaning forward whispered, hoarsely: 'Don't be sarcastic, pray. That's what I've come about.'

When he had grown a little calmer, and tossed off a few bottles of champagne, which we keep in profusion on the dress— we mean sideboard in our sanctum, he said:

'Just before we left England, and just after the Australian Eleven had achieved its great victory at the Oval, some of the English papers, as you are doubtless aware, said that the Australians carried away the ashes of English cricket with them. I referred to this in your Town Hall, the other day, when we arrived, and I added that we had come out to try and take those ashes back again.'

'Right, dear Bligh,' we interjected, 'we remember these facts perfectly well.'

His face grew a shade darker, and there was a decided drooping of his handsome moustaches, as he braced himself up for what was evidently a painful effort.

'I need not tell you, Mr Punch,' he continued, 'that this week we met the Australian Eleven and were beaten by nine wickets.'

'And so,' we said, smiling, 'there was the first good chance gone wrong, of taking back those revered ashes to the old country.'

'Too true,' sighed our visitor, sadly.

'But if you were defeated,' we said, 'you were by no means disgraced. You had very bad luck in having to go in on a bad wicket.'

'No,' said the Hon Ivo, 'that cock won't fight – or, rather, variations of luck are cocks that fight in every cricket match. On the bad wicket we made 177, and next day, going in fresh, and without being fagged by fielding, we only made 169; so we'll say nothing about the luck, if you please. But I have come here for another purpose than to talk of past defeats. I want your honest advice.'

'All right, me dear Bligh,' we replied, in Major Smith's airy style; 'you shall have it.'

'We have lost this match,' said the English captain. 'We play two matches more, and I am not sanguine of winning them. We shall do our level best, of course, but, between ourselves, I think the Australian Eleven is just a little too good for us. Now if –' He hesitated, in evident emotion, and we could perceive that drops of excited perspiration were coursing one another o'er his brow.

'Yes, if –' we repeated, to reassure him. 'Proceed.'

'If we are b-b-beaten, what's to b-b-become of the sususakred –'

'Ashes of English cricket – eh?'

'Precisely.'

'Oh, they'll be all right,' we answered. 'We'll take care of them. The ashes of the fathers couldn't be in better possession than in that of the sturdy sons.'

'I am now coming to the important point,' said the Hon Ivo. 'I regard it as very unlikely that we can get hold of the sacred ashes by fair means this trip. Do you think that, under the extreme circumstances, we would be justified in adopting a different method? I'm told Murdoch has the ashes in a gold snuff-box, which he wears hanging over that great heart, upon which will be found engraved, after his death, The Greatest Batsman of the World, and jam! Do you think that British patriotism would justify us in waylaying Murdoch some dark night, knocking him down and taking the ashes away from him?'

'No,' we replied, firmly. 'We are shocked to hear you mention such a thing. Honourable, we didn't think you'd ha' done it.'

The young man was much moved as he said:

'You are right, Mr Punch, it was a foolish idea. But oh! If you only knew how the people of England treasured those sacred ashes. Many hundreds of cricketers in the old country don't believe that Murdoch's team took them away. I say, if you knew how we treasured them you would pardon me for my weakness.'

He rose dejectedly and prepared to take his leave. It cut us to the heart to see how affected he was, and we pitied him from the bottom of our heart.

As this satire shows, the subject of ashes had quickly become common currency. All they needed now was embodiment, an embodiment which could be seen by the public eye, not only by the inhabitants of Rupertswood.

*   *   *

On 7 January, in a letter home to his father, Bligh summarised his own and his team's position in rather more optimistic terms than the Australian *Punch* had used.

Criterion Hotel
Launceston
Tasmania
Jan 7th 83
My dear Father,
My letter by the last mail was rather taken up by one topic as indeed all my thoughts have been lately. I am much afraid that the finish of our New Year's day match must have been wrongly telegraphed. I have asked Cobbett about it and he is at a loss to account for it altogether.

Bligh, however, was not as downhearted as some England captains have been after a defeat in the opening Test. Len Hutton was to think about throwing himself into the Brisbane River after going 1-0 down in 1954/55. Whether he was buoyed by romantic thoughts or not, Bligh's letter thereafter struck a cheerful tone in describing the mood of his party after their nine-wicket defeat in Melbourne.

We are not in the least daunted and all in the best of spirits and generally jolly. I am getting stronger every day and can stand the cricket in the hot sun without inconvenience. We are just commencing our Tasmanian trip with a wet Sunday at Launceston. It is a pretty little place and the river down which the steamer comes to get to the town is very picturesque. We play tomorrow and the next day, go that night to Hobart 8 hours rail. Then probably Charlie [Studd] and I are going to leave Friday for Melbourne again so as to have another good go at the practice before our next match v Australian XI on the 19th. The others will play in Hobart Friday and Saturday and return to Melbourne Tuesday afternoon.

It did not work out as Bligh had planned. He stayed on in Tasmania for the second game, instead of returning early to Melbourne, and it was as well he did. In Hobart his team came up against the former Australian Test spinner Tom Kendall, and they only reached 110 thanks to the captain opening the innings and top-scoring with 32. His contribution was enough to set up a seven-wicket win, which was well received by the spiritual forerunners of the Barmy Army. Or, as the captain recorded in *Lillywhite's*: 'Among the spectators were to be noticed a strong body of "Jack Tars" from

HMS *Nelson*, whose sympathy with their countrymen was noisily and frequently manifested.'

In his letter home, Bligh wrote:

> I am feeling as you may imagine in a rather perturbed state just now, and I suppose I shall continue to do so until the letter or telegram from you comes in answer to my letter. I do hope you have not thought that I have been rash or hasty in this or that I do not know my own mind. I am quite determined to do anything sooner than give up Miss Morphy and I think when that is the case although you might not be able to do much for me at any rate you would not withhold your permission. I am quite ready to work hard and Miss Morphy will not expect much, indeed she has had too sad an experience in that way to want much. But if you knew the girl I am sure you would say at once that to win such a prize would be a far surer way of obtaining real happiness than any other. If only I could see you and mother and talk it over with you I think you would not think me mistaken whatever you do now.

After the soothing trip to Tasmania Bligh did take something else back to the mainland with him, besides his improving form and romantic yearnings. The Governor of Tasmania was Sir George Strahan, after whom the town in the west of the island on Macquarie Harbour is named. Strahan gave the English captain a lucky penny – 'with the express purpose of defeating Murdoch, a well known favourite of fortune in this respect' according to Bligh's report in *Lillywhite's*. Soon enough, on the morning of 19 January at the MCG, Bligh would find out whether he was going to be as lucky in cricket as he thought he was in love.

Before then, however, came a diplomatic incident or, more precisely, a souped-up press incident: not the first and certainly not the last. Bligh had accepted an invitation from Mr J.W. Bruce to attend a picnic at Fern Glen in the Dandenong Hills two days before the second international match. The Australians had also been invited and, as they were together as a team for a fortnight while the English were in Tasmania, they accepted and went. Bligh, however, having accepted, decided that his team needed a day of practice at the MCG, not picnicking in the hills. Bligh was widely criticised for his rudeness in pulling out of this social engagement at such short notice. But he was to have the last laugh within the week, for after the Second Test the Australians were to be castigated by their newspapers for 'drinking champagne in the bush' before the match, when they should have been practising as England did.

*   *   *

We tend to assume that Test matches between England and Australia are more intense now than they have ever been, as if the increasing amounts of money at stake, in contracts, prizes and sponsorship deals, have caused the increase in intensity. It would be wrong, however, to assume that the Ashes Tests of the nineteenth century were lukewarm and lacklustre, after-you-Claude affairs. After all, there was no other international sporting fixture competing for public attention, and no other way in which to compare England and Australia, the Mother Country and the Colonies, and the merits of their respective manhoods. Cricket seems to have played as much of a part in the newspapers, and in Anglo-Australian (as opposed to Irish-Australian) society, as it does now.

When the 1882/83 series of international matches – originally scheduled to be three in number – moved towards their climax, any intensity which may have been missing from the opening encounter in Melbourne was made good. The cause was not only the English win in the second match, much against the expectations of the Australian *Punch*, which put the outcome of the series back in doubt. There were also allegations of unfair play, made by both sides; and nothing through the ages has increased the tension on and off the field so much as the accusation of cheating. 'There are two teams out there, but only one of them is playing cricket' said Bill Woodfull, as Australia's captain, to Sir Pelham Warner, the manager of Douglas Jardine's team; the intensity of the 1932/33 'Bodyline series' could not have been less than that of the 2005 Ashes series. And physical violence between the two sides, sparked by accusations of cheating, never broke out during the Bodyline series or subsequently, as it appears to have done in the 1882/83 series.

In the Second Test the coin presented by Sir George Strahan worked. Bligh won the toss, batted first on a pitch that was fast and true after plenty of hot sunshine, and saw his side make almost exactly the same total – 294 – that Australia had made when they had batted first in the opening Test (291). Palmer continued his fine off-spin by bowling both of England's opening batsmen, but thereafter Leslie, Steel, Read, Barnes and Bates all made starts, of which Read's 75 was the highest innings. If Leslie and Steel 'gave it away', they had the excuse of stomach upsets.

When Steel wrote the chapter on bowling in the *Cricket* volume of the Badminton library, and talked about the effectiveness of 'breakbacks' or fast off-breaks, he cited Read as an exponent of what he called the golden rule of batting: 'Never allow space between the bat and the left leg for the ball to pass through.' But the 1880s, when Steel wrote this chapter (probably 1887), were such an early stage in the evolution of batting that he went on:

It is an astounding fact that this simple rule, which should be patent to everyone, seems unknown to all our best batsmen with one or two notable exceptions. W.G. Grace has always played with his leg up to the bat, thereby preventing the ball from finding an opening between the two. W.W. Read, of Surrey, is another who plays thus.

And that was Steel's list of the English batsmen of his time who played forward with bat and pad together. Steel also names Read as one of three exponents of a stroke which he calls the pull but posterity would call the sweep. The batsman, he says,

waits till the bowler slightly overtosses a ball – whether pitched outside the off stump or on the wicket he cares not; he sweeps it round to square-leg, where no fieldsman stands, and he makes four runs by the hit. In other words, he deliberately 'pulls' it . . . W.W. Read, H.V. Page, and A.J. Webbe, are all masters of this stroke, which revives the drooping attention of the crowd and relieves the monotony of the scorers.

Was E.W. Swanton, the longstanding correspondent of the *Daily Telegraph*, aware of the stroke's amateur origins when he stigmatised the sweep as 'the bane of English batting'?

The subsequent inquests laid a lot of blame on the Australian selectors – the Melbourne match committee – for omitting Harry Boyle and going into the Second Test with only four frontline bowlers. Then, as in more recent times, Australia's format was six batsmen, four bowlers and a wicketkeeper-batsman. But Tom Garrett was not penetrative, and Spofforth was not in good form, leaving all ten of England's wickets to be taken by the two off-spinners, Palmer and George Giffen. Australia's fielding for once was poor, or, as the *Melbourne Age* reported: 'in batting and fielding especially there was a marked falling off from the brilliancy which has on all previous occasions characterised the champions' play . . . It is quite a new experience to have to record that Blackham behind the wickets was not quite himself, but such was the case in the match just finished.'

It is an indication of the high standard of fielding in the early 1880s that Spofforth was not thought to be worthy of any great praise when he picked up at extra-cover and threw the stumps down at the bowler's end before Leslie could complete a single. Much, however, was made of the mistake by Tom Horan, after Read had cut a ball and the non-striker Barnes had called for a single. Read did not move, and Barnes joined him in the batsman's crease, but Horan made such a wild return that Barnes regained his ground. Another report mentions that the bowler, Spofforth, fell over the stumps in trying to take Horan's throw.

Read and Barnes took England's score to 195 for four before a minor collapse. Barnes, like the openers, was clean bowled by an off-break, this time from Giffen, as was Tylecote, who kept his batting form well through the tour considering he had nobody to share the wicketkeeping. So too was Bligh, bowled Giffen 0; was the captain's bat again not vertical in defence? The score of 199 for seven would have been worse still if Bates had not been dropped first ball when he drove Giffen to long-off, the culprit being Horan again.

Bates might have sensed that it was going to be his day, if not the match of his life. In Giffen's next over, he drove two fours and a 2: 10 runs off four balls. Read joined in, and benefited from a missed stumping by Blackham when he had made 42; it would have been 216 for eight had this chance been taken, with only George Studd – long since dropped down the order – and Morley to come. This was Australia's last chance to restrict England to a manageable first-innings total. The home side failed to seize it, so that England went to the close of play at 248 for seven.

The crowd on the first day at the MCG, a Friday, was no more than 6,000. The New Year holidays were over, and the general expectation had been that Australia would win again easily. On the second day, with Australia up against it, 'One of Them' reported:

> the ring presented a much more respectable appearance, and there were quite 15,000 present. On Saturday afternoons all the large business establishments in the city close at two o'clock, and large numbers avail themselves of the recognised half-holiday to indulge, during the summer season, in all kinds of outdoor sports, in which cricket plays a leading part. It is for this reason that all grand matches, such as the one under notice, are commenced on a Friday, in order that the most interesting portion of the play may fall on the Saturday afternoon, and thus attract a large proportion of pleasure-seekers, for it cannot be denied that, equally with England, cricket is the national pastime of Australia, and first-class exhibitions of the game will always attract large and enthusiastic crowds of spectators.

By more vigorous hitting Read and Bates took their eighth wicket stand up to 88 and the England total to 287 for seven before the innings folded for 294. Palmer took the last three wickets, Bates being caught at long-off by Horan, who had earlier dropped him while fielding in the same position. This left the Australians with a brief session before lunch, and broke up the day nicely for Bligh's team, who were also helped by some overcast weather, which not only made bowling and fielding cooler work: it was also remarked that catching was easier, at least for the English players, on cloudy days in Australia than on bright sunny days.

Whether the conditions helped them or not, it is certain that when Australia batted England rose to the occasion and turned on their best bowling and out-cricket. The *Melbourne Argus* was to say after the match: 'It is no exaggeration to say that such fielding as they exhibited has never been seen on an Australian ground before, and the bowling was of the first class also. Every nerve was strained by the Eleven. The players were strung up to concert pitch.' Such a tribute speaks volumes for Bligh's captaincy and the morale of his team. It also speaks well of Tylecote as the wicketkeeper who orchestrated the fielding. Tylecote, moreover, had to take over the captaincy on the second day after lunch, when Bligh retired with lumbago. The captain returned on the Monday, and fielded well himself.

All the skill of England's fielding was needed as Hugh Massie began with another spectacular assault. The previous summer the *Daily Telegraph* in London had said that Massie was 'as shapely as a greyhound' and he could score as quickly as one could run. Australia were 19 for no wicket after three overs, in other words after 12 balls. Charles Studd's first three overs were hit for 22, all by Massie. At lunch Massie had scored 26 while Alec Bannerman had yet to get off the mark. After lunch Massie continued until he was bowled by Barlow for 43 out of 56 for one. Not quite as devastating as his counter-attack at the Oval had been, but he had still given Australia the momentum.

Momentum which their captain Billy Murdoch then proceeded to lose. He came in to partner Bannerman, Alec the Australian stonewaller, and together they let England bowl. After Bannerman had scored a few runs off his own bat, eight maidens were bowled before any addition to the total, and this addition came from four byes. Fourteen consecutive maidens were bowled in all by Morley, Barlow and Bates before Murdoch scored his first run. Morley was still not fit, and below his normal pace, but he still bowled 23 overs in the innings for only 13 runs. Murdoch appeared to acknowledge that his tactics had been wrong in his first innings by batting far more positively in his second, but by then he was too late.

To England's aid a sharp shower also came. Play was not halted, but some considered the rain had enlivened the pitch. Whether it was or not, Bannerman was bowled by Bates, who had come on at the end opposite the pavilion and who was to bowl, with only the briefest break, until the end of the match. Horan immediately hit Bates to square leg for 3 – his obvious intention to regain the initiative which Massie had secured – then straight-drove the other off-spinner Barnes hard and straight, only for the bowler to stick up a hand and make 'an exceedingly good catch', according to 'One of Them'.

Percy McDonnell came in to join Murdoch, doctor and solicitor together. Of the six Test centuries made until this point, McDonnell's had arguably been the finest, surpassing those of Murdoch, W.G. Grace, Ulyett, Horan and Charles Bannerman, who had made his 165 in the inaugural Test when the England players had been finding their feet after their voyage from New Zealand. McDonnell had scored 147 in the Third Test of 1881/82, on a very bad Sydney pitch: in Australia's total of 260 Alex Bannerman scored 70, nobody else reached double figures, and their stand of 199 – the highest in Test cricket until 1884 – set up a six-wicket win. But here McDonnell, after cutting Barnes for 3, was bowled by Bates. Australia, who had been 72 for one, had slumped to 78 for four, and their prospects were, like the light, going from bad to worse. And neither end at the MCG in those days had a sightscreen.

Giffen came out in the murk and pushed his first ball straight back to Bates, who was thus on a hat-trick, not that one had ever been taken by an England bowler before. Next came Bonnor, at number seven, the position where he had cracked 85 to win the First Test. Then, as now, the convention at every level of the game was to crowd the batsman for the hat-trick ball and England, although Bligh was not there to dictate, did so. A little psychology was involved too. For all the fine, strong batsmen since, it can be easily argued that Bonnor was the hardest hitter of a cricket ball that Australia has ever produced. On the tour of England in 1880 he hit a ball 147 yards from hit to pitch. In practice at the MCG Bonnor made hits of 150 yards and 160 yards, according to Jack Pollard in his authoritative work *Australian Cricket: The Game and the Players*. 'Bonnor was a born hitter' his team-mate George Giffen wrote. 'He had a distinct mission as a demoraliser of bowlers and fieldsmen and if he had always adhered to the strict terms of his commission he would have made a great many more runs.' But Bonnor wanted to be more than a Bathurst country boy who slogged. According to Pollard: 'His weakness was his yearning to be regarded as an elegant, stylish batsman. Often he went to the wicket determined to prove he was not just a big hitter, but these quests for orthodoxy were invariably frustrated.'

If Bonnor had consistently played his natural game, no fielder would have stood close for him without a helmet, shin guards and other protection. England sensed he would not play his natural game, at least for the hat-trick ball. In Badminton *Cricket,* Allan Steel wrote:

> Somebody suggested that, in the faint hope of securing a 'hat' for Bates, we should try a silly mid-on. Bates faithfully promised to bowl a fast shortish ball between the legs and the wicket, and said he was quite certain that Bonnor would play slowly forward to it. Acting on the faith of this, W.W. Read boldly volunteered to stand silly mid-on for one ball. In came the giant – loud were the shouts of welcome from the larrikins' throats; now would the ball soar over the green trees even higher than yonder flock of twittering parrots. As Bates began to walk to the wickets to bowl, nearer and nearer crept our brave mid-on; a slow forward stroke to a fast shortish leg-stump ball landed the ball in his hands not more than six feet from the bat. The crowd would not believe it and Bonnor was simply thunderstruck at mid-on's impertinence; but Bates had done the hat-trick for all that, and what is more, he got a very smart silver hat for his pains.

Bates, of course, always dressed smartly.

It was the second hat-trick in Test cricket, following Spofforth's on the same ground in 1879. But the Australian's had been taken against the motley combination under Lord Harris billed as 'Gentlemen of England (with Ulyett and Emmett)'. Of Spofforth's hat-trick victims, one was Emmett, who was more of a bowler; another was the Reverend Vernon Royle, who had four initials and a first-class career batting average of 15; and the third was Francis MacKinnon, who did not make the first XI at Harrow, also averaged 15 in his first-class career and would surely never have come near an England side if he had not been the 35th MacKinnon of MacKinnon. Neither Royle nor MacKinnon was selected for another international match. (The MacKinnon however lived to become the oldest Test cricketer until he died 40 days short of his 99th birthday, wearing to the end on his watch-chain a gold medallion bearing an insignia of crossed bats which had been presented to the members of Harris's team.)

Bligh, in his account for *Lillywhite's*, did not refer to any rain enlivening the pitch, but chose to think that the dismissals of Bannerman and Horan had set up the Australian middle order for Bates. 'The sudden downfall of two or three of their best wickets seemed to have paralysed the play of the succeeding batsmen, and MacDonnell, Giffen, and Bonnor fell to successive balls, thus earning Bates the right to a hat, which was duly presented to him, in commemoration of this most remarkable feat.' Murdoch's defensiveness played its part too. When Australia were all out not long afterwards for 114, Murdoch was left undefeated with 19 runs scored in two and a half hours. Only two blemishes had marred England's out-cricket, apart from four overthrows: one was a missed catch at point by Steel before Murdoch had scored, and the second a chance to Tylecote off a bouncing off-break from Bates, but it cost nothing as Palmer was yorked straight afterwards by Bates.

It was in Australia's second innings that the controversy began. Bates's first-innings haul of seven for 28 was explicable in that Australia, especially Murdoch, batted so defensively that they let him get on top; in that the light became difficult for batting; and in that rain freshened the pitch (although certain English sources did not mention it, 'One of Them' was sufficiently candid to say the pitch became 'somewhat treacherous'). But once the pitch had been rolled, and the light had improved, and Australia – and Murdoch in particular – had changed their approach, none of these explanations applied. Yet Bates still took seven wickets in Australia's second innings.

Following on at half-past five on the Saturday afternoon, 180 runs behind, Australia reached 28 for one at stumps. Murdoch was the man out, for 17, bowled by Bates after hitting him to square leg and setting a more aggressive example – although the man he replaced as opener, Massie, would have been still more attacking. No rain fell over the Sunday. On Monday, the third day, 'the ground was therefore in fair order, and the day, though cloudy, was bright and clear, with plenty of light for both batting and fielding' wrote 'One of Them'.

Australia's night-watchman, Blackham, was bowled first ball by Barlow, who started the bowling from the pavilion end, while Bates continued from the railway end. And it was Barlow, the sober Lancastrian, who prompted the controversy and the accusations of unfair play. He wore studs in his bowling boots – studs which had raked the mud out of the bowler's footholds at the Oval a few months before. Studs which some Australians thought made holes in the pitch for Bates, from the other end, to pitch into.

First, though, England had their hands full with Bonnor, who was promoted to number four and to hit Bates out of the attack. Bonnor duly hit him to leg for four and, next ball, over the chains for five; Bannerman meanwhile had not added to his overnight score of 5. Bonnor then hit Bates for five a second time and a third, 'over the heads of the spectators' according to 'One of Them'. Bligh took off Bates and brought on Morley opposite Barlow. The total had shot up to 55 for two: still plenty of runs to play with, provided Bonnor did not last an hour or two, and he did not. Bonnor was gone with the score on 66 when he hit the ever-steady Barlow to mid-on.

Bligh instantly brought Bates back in place of Morley, and the Yorkshireman ran through the rest of Australia's second innings. At lunch Australia were 122 for seven, and Giffen was dismissed soon afterwards when he cut Bates 'hard to point and was beautifully caught by Bligh' ('One of Them'). Garrett hit Bates to Barnes at long-off, while Palmer hit Bates to mid-off, where George Studd had been the pick of the fielders throughout. According to the *Age*:

The only unpleasant feature in the match was a cowardly attempt made by a small knot of roughs to prevent Barnes catching Garrett, by jeering at the fieldsman as he was preparing for the catch. But that these small souled fellows were alone in their unmanly behaviour was clearly evinced by the hearty, even boisterous way in which the mass of spectators cheered the winners. Every member of the team was called forth on to the pavilion balcony and cheered to the echo, Bates, of course, coming in for a great ovation. Mr Bligh was so impressed by this generous treatment that he declared to his friends inside that a finer acknowledgment of victory could not have been accorded an English team by English people on English ground.

Lots of big shots had been attempted, in vain. Nevertheless, the Australians accused Barlow in his follow-through of cutting up the pitch, and making holes in it, into which Bates pitched his off-breaks. The *Age* dismissed it: 'As to the Australians' batting, its failure has been ascribed to the wicket assisting the bowling of Bates to an unusual degree. The excuse is quite an imaginary one, and the brilliancy of Bates' wonderful performance should not be tarnished by such assertions.'

Something was fishy on the statistical surface, however. Bates took fourteen wickets in the Test for 104 runs, yet in the other six first-class matches on tour he took only seven more wickets. Bligh's choice of Bates to bowl ahead of Barnes and opposite Barlow was interesting in itself. In the *Cricket* volume of the Badminton library, Steel wrote that the ideal 'medium-pace right round-arm bowler' was Barnes 'with his nasty awkward action, his break-back, and the kicky nature of his bowling on almost all wickets'. But for the pitch at the MCG in this game Bligh preferred Bates who was, in Steel's estimation, a slow off-spinner. It must have been the fuller length which Bates offered that was attractive to Bligh, a length which would have landed in Barlow's footmarks whereas Barnes' natural length, surely, was short of them.

The upshot came before the Third Test at Sydney when Murdoch spoke to Bligh. Australia's captain complained to England's captain about the studs which Barlow was using in his boots. Barlow protested that they were exactly the same bowling boots and studs that he used in county cricket. Bligh, not willing to be confrontational with Murdoch, told Barlow to remove his studs, and the bowler did so. Bligh, however, did not ask Murdoch to tell Spofforth to change or remove his studs; England's captain no doubt preferred a quiet life to confrontation.

The Third Test, however, did not work out quietly. The scoreline now stood at one-all and everybody was saying the third international match in Sydney would be the decider for the Ashes. It proved to be one of the most combustible of all Test matches.

2. Ivo at Cheam. As he appears happy enough, he must have established himself on the school cricket field.

1. Young Ivo by Lewis Carroll, who was able to make every child he photographed think they were his favourite; they became absolutely fearless in his company. 'We felt he was one of us, and on our side against all the grown-ups.'

4. Florence Rose aged 5. She most likely would have had a slight Australian lilt to her voice but this was soon lost on coming to England.

3. Ivo at Eton – the only surviving photograph of him in cricket flannels.

5. Ivo, sitting, with his lifelong friend the Hon. Alfred Lyttelton at Cambridge. They were the University's first rackets pair in 1880, and remained unbeaten.

6. According to the profile of the Sixth Earl of Darnley, Ivo's father, in *Vanity Fair*, 'he is not a very brilliant man, but he is an excellent husband, a popular land-lord, and a real aristocrat of the old style … Like Lady Darnley he is full of charity, holding that the principal object of life is to do good. He owns Cobham Hall, in which fine place he has earned great reputation for the luxuriant variety of his rhododendrons.'

7. Portraits of Murdoch's 1882 Australians.

HUGH HAMON MASSIE

WILLIAM LLOYD MURDOCH
(Captain)

GEORGE JOHN BONNER

FREDERICK ROBERT SPOFFORTH

JOHN M'CARTHY BLACKHAM

SAMUEL PERCY JONES

ALEXANDER CHAMBERS BANNERMAN

GEORGE EUGENE PALMER

PERCY STANISLAUS M'DONNELL

THOMAS WILLIAM GARRETT

HENRY FREDERICK BOYLE

CHARLES WILLIAM BEAL
(Secretary)

GEORGE GIFFIN

THOMAS HORAN

GRAND CRICKET MATCH, *played in* Lord's *Ground* Mary-le-bone, *on June 20, following day, between the* EARLS *of* WINCHELSEA & DARNLEY *for 1000 Guineas.*

8. The Fourth Earl of Darnley, also Kent captain, led his own XI in this match on Thomas Lord's first ground. Only two stumps are shown, though the three-stump wicket was introduced in the 1770s.

9. 'Some Famous Living Cricketers', published in 1883. Ivo is behind W.G. Grace and Lord Harris, but had he carried on playing cricket after his tour, he would not have faded into the background.

10. W.G. Grace. One of the earlier photographs of the most famous of all English cricketers, a super-athlete in physique and self-confidence.

11. Scorecard of the Oval Test of 1882. No bowling analyses were recorded, so Spofforth's feat of taking 14 wickets for 90 runs does not get a mention.

12. Florence (left) and Janet, Lady Clarke (right) photographed in 1884 just prior to Florence's marriage to Ivo. The intimacy suggested in the pose is that of younger and older sister.

13. Florence in the 1890s, before becoming Countess of Darnley, and when she was still trying to find a fulfilling role.

14. The Colombo cricket ground in 1889. Barlow reported that some members of the local side, of European origin, played in bare feet. The Studd brothers no doubt visited the church as well.

15. As Cambridge University captain in 1881, Ivo had written to the Melbourne Cricket Club proposing a tour of Australia, which was duly approved. Major Benjamin Wardill was secretary of the Melbourne club for 32 years, having kept wicket for them, and managed several Australian tours of England. His elder brother Richard was also born in Lancashire but met a stickier end: after hitting the first century in Australian first-class cricket, for Victoria against New South Wales in 1867, he confessed to stealing £7,000 from his employers, the Victorian Sugar Company, and drowned himself in the River Yarra aged 38.

Melbourne Cricket Club.

Offices: 1 Exchange,
Melbourne, 4th January, 1882.

A SPECIAL GENERAL MEETING of the Club will be held in the New Pavilion, on Wednesday, 11th instant, at 4 p.m., when a proposal from the HON. IVO BLIGH, to bring out a Team of English Cricketers to Australia during next Season, will be considered.

Yours faithfully,

B. J. WARDILL, Secretary.

POST CARD

The Address only to be written on this side.

To G. Wilkie Esq

C Collins St E

16. Fred Morley, the simple soul who was badly injured on the voyage out and who died within the year.

17. William Murdoch: scorer of the first double-century in Test cricket, 211 at the Oval in 1884, and the first triple-century in Australia, 321 for New South Wales against Victoria in 1881/82.

19. Alexander Bannerman, the younger, shorter and more defensive of the two brothers who opened the batting for Australia.

18. George, or 'Joey', Palmer, Australia's form bowler in the 1882/83 series with his off-spin. In 1886 he became the first Australian to do the double of 1,000 runs and 100 wickets on a first-class tour of England.

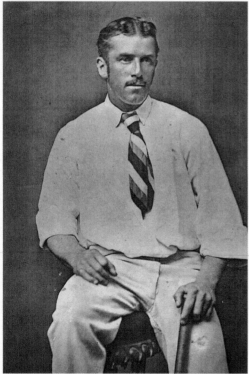

20. Albert Hornby, or 'O my Hornby' as Francis Thompson hailed him, was the captain of Lancashire, and of England in the 1882 Test.

21. Richard Barlow, England's answer to Alexander Bannerman as a stonewaller, and more besides as he was also a fine slow-medium, non-spinning left-armer.

22. William Barnes, once a lad and always a lad, the archetypal professional cricketer of the 1880s.

23. Jack Blackham, the first great wicket-keeper, played more Tests than any other cricketer of the nineteenth century (35).

7

The Ashes Regained

Among the half-dozen most controversial matches ever played between England and Australia, the Third Test at Sydney of 1882/83 has to be ranked. The series stood at one-all. The Ashes, for the first time, were at stake, although only as a metaphor rather than a physical prize. Accusations of unfair play, by both sides, heightened the tension. Only if the series had been standing at two-all in a five-Test series of full dramatic potential, and if W.G. Grace had arrived as a late replacement, could the intensity have been greater.

The two teams had sailed on the same ship from Melbourne to Sydney directly the Second Test had finished in England's favour. Bligh was still in a state of anxiety about whether his father would grant him permission to marry Florence Morphy, indigent as she was. His letter home would take at least six weeks to reach his father, and then, after the stern old patriarch had sat on the balcony outside his bedroom in the morning air and read his Bible, what would his reaction to the letter be? Bligh would have to wait a few more days, beyond the six weeks, before his father's reply reached Australia. At the earliest it would be late February before he received the telegram with the succinct message he longed for: BLIGH CRICKET AUSTRALIA YES DARNLEY. Not that it ever arrived.

In the meantime the other great matter in Bligh's life was soon going to be resolved, for better or worse, for richer or poorer, but only after a fight to the death which spread over five days, including a Sunday. The physical togetherness of the two teams on board ship from Melbourne did not generate any harmony that lasted once they disembarked in Sydney. Lord Harris had been roughed up during a game there on his 1878/79 tour, but that was not in a Test match, and he was struck by spectators, not players. The players in the Sydney Test of 1882/83 appear to have come closer to physically violent contact on the field than in any Test match before or since.

In public – in his speeches during the tour and in his match report for *Lillywhite's* – Bligh was a model of discretion. In the latter he contented himself with one small, dry, reference to the fact that Tom Horan, an occasional medium-pacer who took 35 wickets in his first-class career, was turned almost into a match-winner by Spofforth's tendency to run down the pitch in his follow-through and cut it up. 'Our second innings, though it began fairly well, fell away sadly towards the end, the wicket being cut up at both ends by Spofforth's heels to such an extent that Horan became an unplayable bowler; perhaps, if we would, we could say no more than that.' In private, however, in his letters home to his father, Bligh came as close as he ever did in his correspondence to losing his temper.

During the Second Test in Melbourne the ill feeling generated by Spofforth and Barlow, and by the impact which their studs had on the pitch, had been kept within the bounds of restraint. The lid came off on the afternoon of 25 January 1883, the day before the Third Test, when after practice at the SCG Billy Murdoch protested to Bligh about Barlow's studs and demanded that they be removed. The Australian correspondent of the *Argus* who saw Barlow's boots and studs described them as 'heavy steel blades fastened across the sole of the boot'. For the *Sportsman*, Cobbett described the spikes as 'small clamps', the same as Barlow had worn in England the previous season, with which he had scraped mud out of the bowler's footholds at the Oval.

In his letter home after the Test, Bligh told his father:

We had rather a stormy discussion in Sydney about cutting up the wicket by bowlers' feet. At Murdoch's request Barlow changed his spikes. As Spofforth had been a byword in England for cutting up the wicket for the bowler at the other end this was a pretty strong measure – but when Murdoch in reward for this courtesy on our part put Spofforth on to bowl both ends and cut up the wicket more disgracefully than I have ever seen done before our fellows were naturally very angry about it.

Stormy, disgracefully, very angry: this was an English aristocrat speaking, one born to understatement, yet this is the vocabulary of today's most lurid tabloids.

The controversy was caused by a grey area in the laws which both teams, in accordance with human nature at its most competitive, tried to exploit to the full – England in Melbourne and Australia in Sydney. At the time the issue of a bowler running on the pitch and damaging it came under the Law which specified, then as now, that the umpires are the sole judges of fair and unfair play. England's accusation was that what Spofforth *did* was unfair in that he cut up the pitch and thus helped the bowler at the opposite end. Spofforth's defence was that he did not *intend* to cut up the pitch and therefore could not be accused of unfair play. Any damage was simply a natural consequence of his bowling action, which began from an angle almost as wide as mid-off, and his follow-through down the pitch – a vigorous follow-through, given the sweep of his right hand which almost touched the ground. The umpires at the time, Messrs Swift and Elliott in the first three Tests, ruled in Spofforth's favour.

The value of the testimony of an independent witness – a professional journalist, not a player on either side – was borne out by Cobbett's account of the match. In the *Sportsman* he reported that Spofforth 'made a hole for himself to pitch into, returned, and, with Horan for partner, quickly got rid of his opponents'. This hole was 'an area about a foot by 18 inches scraped into ridges, making the surface uneven to the extent of a couple of inches, and causing the ball dropped on to them to be nearly unplayable.' He added that Spofforth hardly needed spikes to cut up a pitch because 'lately he has adopted a method of screwing his heel into the ground'.

Even so, the lid might have stayed on this controversy if Sydney had provided a firm pitch, such as the players had enjoyed at the MCG, at least when dry. From a running sore the issue was turned into a full-blown row because the pitches at the SCG, as England had found in their warm-up game against New South Wales, were renowned for being loosely compacted: thus they deteriorated far more rapidly than Melbourne's pitches. Indeed the custom was still established at the SCG, when it had died out in England, of preparing two pitches for a match so that the captains when they tossed would not only decide which side would bat first but also which pitch each of them preferred to bat on.

Sydney's first enclosed cricket ground, where the public could be charged for admission, was the Albert ground at Redfern, where the first English tourists played. The ground at Moore Park, which became famous as the SCG, was originally used by the garrison of British troops and only handed over to the New South Wales Cricket Association five years before Bligh's tour. Therefore these were still early days for the SCG groundsmen; and experience has shown that new cricket grounds need several years before their pitches bed down. Otherwise everything in the SCG garden was lovely, according to Cobbett's dispatch for the *Sportsman*:

> It is certainly the finest run-getting ground I have ever seen, and the arrangements of the establishment are exceedingly well devised and carried out. The total area of the field is about twelve acres, of which the space named reserved for play is boarded by an open pale fence about thirty inches high, having (except in front of the pavilion) a foot or so inside it a small ditch, or grip, which constitutes the boundary.

As a player, 'One of Them' was in a better position to offer a close-up of the SCG pitches:

> The turf on the playing ground is covered with a closely grown and small variety of couch grass, which, however, does not produce the same reliable wickets which are to be found when English ryegrass and clover form the component parts of the vegetation. For out-fielding, however, the couch grass is really excellent, and when cut close, the ball travels as on a billiard table. When I say that the wickets are not so good, I do not infer that they are bad, but they have not the same lasting properties as those covered with ryegrass and clover. This difficulty was, however, got over to a very

considerable extent by the arrangement that each side should have their own wicket.

'Got over to a very considerable extent': this is not the verdict of posterity. Posterity has concluded that for a Test match to be a true test of cricket skills, both sides have to bat on the same pitch and therefore be weighed in the same balance. The pitch will deteriorate as a match progresses, or occasionally improve for batting, but it remains the same strip of turf. Whereas if each side bats on a different pitch, perhaps differently prepared, their skills cannot be compared directly.

England, however, batted so badly in the first half of the opening day that they almost lost the game there and then, without controversy. Bligh had won the toss again with the lucky coin presented to him by the Governor of Tasmania, and had no hesitation about batting first on a fine day. But the pressure of the occasion, although such a phrase is an anachronism, would appear to have affected England's top-order batting. The size of the crowd on the opening day was estimated at 23,000 by 'One of Them', being 'the largest ever witnessed at the Moore Park ground'. Stirrings of nationalistic fervour might also have encouraged the Australians and inhibited the Englishmen because it was 26 January 1883, the 95th anniversary of the founding of the colony of New South Wales. The counter-attractions included a regatta on the Parramatta River, racing at Randwick and picnicking around Sydney Harbour, but people came by their thousands to the SCG, even though the seating outside the pavilion and the old Brewongle Stand was temporary.

With the series to be won and lost, England slumped to 76 for five wickets. Charles Studd was caught behind off Tom Garrett, Leslie bowled by a fast yorker from Spofforth, and Barlow caught left-handed by Murdoch at point off Spofforth to round off a satisfactory morning for Australia. Steel was bowled by Garrett straight after lunch, and Barnes caught behind off Spofforth. At this juncture, with England about to waste the toss and their own first-day pitch, the steady Tylecote joined the in-form Read and England's sixth-wicket pair counter-attacked. Tylecote had made a hundred for Kent against the Australians in 1882. Now he became the first wicket-keeper to score a fifty in Test cricket, when the series was in the balance. Tylecote deserves to be known as the first of the line of Kent and England wicketkeeper-batsmen which has continued through Les Ames, Godfrey Evans and Alan Knott to Geraint Jones, all of them prospering in both spheres of the game on the firm pitches of Canterbury.

So rapidly did Read and Tylecote score that Murdoch was forced to look beyond his four-man attack of Spofforth and Garrett, Palmer and Giffen. In an effort to break what turned out to be the decisive partnership of 115, Murdoch turned to his occasional bowlers Bannerman and McDonnell (Horan was not even tried at this stage). The tactic worked, but only thanks to a run-out. In McDonnell's first over Tylecote turned the ball towards square leg, ran, was sent back by Read, and was 'several yards out of his ground' when Horan whipped the ball into Blackham. In the previous Test it had only been a wild throw by Horan which had saved Read from being involved in another run-out, that of Barnes.

Bates maintained the rollicking rate with Read until the latter pulled a long-hop from Bannerman to square leg. He and Tylecote had each contributed 66. 'Read's batting was a fine, vigorous, all-round display' according to 'One of Them'. After Bates had lofted Spofforth to long-on, Bligh came in and made his first batting contribution of the series. His total of 30 runs for once out in a low-scoring match was most timely, but overall England's first-innings total of 247 was not much to write home about in a letter to his father. 'A fair score' was how Bligh summarised it.

'Our catching was, as usual, contemptible.' The decisive Sydney Test provoked some relatively strong language in Bligh, and this phrase was not confined to his private correspondence but was his verdict on England's fielding in *Lillywhite's*. He was referring to the passage of play in Australia's first innings on the Saturday when, after rain overnight and more during the day, Australia took the upper hand and reached the close of play with nine wickets in hand.

Rain falling during the night made the match look all in our favour, but, unluckily, it continued to fall in showers at intervals during the whole day, and our bowlers had to bowl with a wet ball on a cutting-through wicket – result, one wicket only down for 133, a state of things which, for all our bowlers' disadvantages, did Murdoch, Giffen, and Bannerman the greatest credit. Our catching was, as usual, contemptible.

During this passage England dropped four catches. Bligh did not name the offenders in public but he did to his father. 'They [the Australians] certainly had the worst of the luck in the wicket though they made a very good start on a showery day, 133 for one wicket. On that day we very nearly threw our chance away by missing easy catches, Leslie, Morley and Bates being the worst defaulters.' Bates at mid-off dropped Giffen off Barlow; Murdoch, when only 5, hit Bates straight into Leslie's hands at mid-on and was reprieved; Bannerman, when 39, was dropped at short leg by Morley off Bates again. The fourth chance came when Bannerman edged Steel to Barnes at slip. Although the captain did not classify Barnes among the worst defaulters, 'One of Them' said this fourth drop was another 'very bad miss, all of which should certainly have been taken'.

Bligh and his bowlers were lucky to be given a second chance. On the Sunday, a rest day, it rained again and made the uncovered pitch much more difficult than on the showery Saturday. Instead of skidding through, the ball on Monday gripped on turf that was cutting up in Sydney fashion. 'The last 2 days the wicket was caked and very bad to play on' Bligh admitted to his father. England's bowlers were also able to grip the ball better on the Monday – and Bligh, as always, had a wide range of bad-wicket bowlers to choose from. Could Australia push on from 133 for one and take a first-innings lead? A lead of substance would win the match.

This question was not to be resolved quickly. Australia's first innings lasted for 176.3 four-ball overs, or 117.5 six-ball overs. In other words, with the series at stake, and the prize of the Ashes at least in the back of their minds, the Australians fought and fought. But might Murdoch's strategy have been too defensive again? He had a very aggressive batsman in Hugh Massie, and one of the biggest hitters of all time in George Bonnor, and either one or the other might have completely taken the game away from England on the Saturday when the ball was skidding through and greasy for the England bowlers and fielders. Instead, Massie and Bonnor came in at numbers six and seven, too low down to dictate the course of the game. On the Monday, resuming shortly after midday, Bannerman and Murdoch cautiously continued their second-wicket stand, adding three singles in the first six overs. Together they took Australia's first innings up to 140 for one in reply to England's 247; but the weather, the conditions and Australia's tactics were on Bligh's side.

Steel had not done much bowling in the first two Tests, concentrating instead on his batting at four or five, but he chipped in now with three prime wickets: Murdoch lbw, McDonnell clean-bowled, and Massie caught by Bligh at point. In between, Bannerman was caught in the slips – Bates there now, not Barnes – off Morley for 94, a bad-wicket innings which might have won Australia the series if he had been given aggressive support at the other end. Bannerman had made more than half the runs when he was out at 176 for four. With Massie also dismissed at the same score, Australia were 176 for five and it was time for Bonnor. An hour of Bonnor could still turn the match and series.

Sensibly, Bligh kept Morley on because Bonnor's preference was for slower bowling. (At the other end Steel was bowling his off-breaks and odd slower leg-break to Horan.) When Bonnor faced Morley, the giant wound up and smashed the ball skywards behind the bowler – either a vital chance to be held or a fifth chance in Australia's innings to be dropped. If Bligh had time to think, he must have taken some comfort from the observation that his man at mid-off was George Studd. With the bat the older Studd had endured a wretched tour, starting at the top of the order but unable to make runs even in the up-country games, so that he dropped to number nine in the First Test and ten in the second. But he was, all along, Bligh's outstanding fielder, either at mid-off or extra-cover; and he had a grand opportunity to confirm this title when Bonnor hit out and the ball rose above the Sydney Cricket Ground and sailed away towards the mid-off boundary. Studd ran after it and took the hardest type of all outfield catches, the ball coming over his shoulder. 'One of Them', who cannot have been far away, described it as 'a most brilliant catch'. In his four Tests Studd only scored 31 runs at an average of 4, but during the last half-century of his life, spent as a missionary to the poor in downtown Los Angeles, he could have been forgiven the indulgence of closing his eyes and reliving the moment when Bonnor smote in Sydney and he was equal to the giant's strength. In his four Tests George Studd took eight catches, a rate of two per game which has never been matched, let alone bettered, by any England fielder – before or since – who has played more than three Tests.

Australia were all out for 218. England's lead was 29, a small number today perhaps, but crucial in a low-scoring dogfight on a bad pitch when Spofforth had to be faced for a second time. Before England batted again, the pitch on which their first innings had been staged was rolled. But if their pitch was flattened out, it was not for long. Spofforth began the bowling at one end, then switched to the other and bowled into the footmarks he had made. Bligh said his men had travelled 16,000 miles to play Spofforth on a dry wicket, and they were not about to enjoy that experience.

Instead, it was the same old story: Spofforth up to all his tricks on a pitch which he himself had cut up; Spofforth bowling unchanged through an innings; Spofforth bowling England out. His second-innings bowling figures in Sydney were exactly the same as they had been at the Oval: seven wickets for 44. He clean-bowled three of England's top four batsmen as England collapsed to 98 for eight before an important late flurry from Bligh, who was incensed by the state of the pitch, judging by his letter home. 'Spofforth cut up the wicket in no time with his feet' he wrote, before commenting that he had done it 'more disgracefully than I have ever seen done before'. Earlier, after Read had gone after Garrett, Murdoch turned to Horan for some medium-pace and the part-timer supplied it, benefiting sufficiently from the 'preparations' by Spofforth to record his best figures of three wickets for 22.

The difference between Sydney in 1883 and the Oval in 1882 was that England now had the runs on the board, 123 of them to go with their first-innings lead, setting Australia 153 to win on the fourth morning, a Tuesday; and again Australia were over-defensive. They began with their four most stubborn batsmen against the two left-armers, Morley and Barlow, and to little effect as the four were out with 18 runs on the board – a scoreboard which had been brought up from the MCG as it was so detailed, showing everything except the bowling figures. All momentum had gone out of Australia's bid for victory by the time Massie and Bonnor came together at 30 for five. The English bowlers were well on top and the fielding was holding firm under the influence of Bligh, who took three catches himself in the game, one of them 'splendidly caught' ('One of Them'). Blackham's skills as a bad-wicket left-handed batsman were evident in the first innings, when he scored 27, but he was never going to score quickly enough to win the match himself, given the rate of wickets falling at the other end. It had to be Massie or Bonnor, if not both, who propelled Australia to the finishing line. And when Massie was caught by Charles Studd behind cover-point, and Bonnor clean bowled by Barlow, England's relief can be imagined. Their winning margin of 69 runs was not by any means so comfortable as it sounds.

'There was massive enthusiasm and I was very nearly torn to pieces by the crowd afterwards' Bligh told his father. 'There was an enormous attendance in spite of the bad weather.' According to the *Australasian*:

> the Hon Ivo Bligh was called forth by the crowd, and each of his associates had to follow in ordinary course to bow acknowledgments to the enthusiastic lookers-on. On their way to the luncheon room too, the Britishers had to face a perfect storm of plaudits, and Barlow, owing to his very successful bowling, had the honour of being carried shoulder high by the excited crowd right into the luncheon room itself. The Hon Ivo Bligh too had his hand shaken nearly off by many enthusiastic well-wishers, and altogether it seemed as if those present had fully made up their minds to duly appreciate the victory of the Englishmen.

Bligh continued in his letter home: 'Telegrams of congratulation have poured in from every part. Did I tell you that Sir George Strahan, Governor of Tasmania, gave me a lucky shilling with which I won the toss in both these last matches? When the news of our victory reached Hobart where the men-of-war are the result was flashed all round the fleet by night signals!'

The post-match exchanges were not, however, all friendly sweetness and cordial light. Far from it. Piecing together the various versions, each one veiled in Victorian discretion, and coming to a precise conclusion more than a century afterwards, is impossible. But the evidence suggests there was pushing and shoving, and perhaps blows were exchanged between the protagonists as they walked off the field.

Australia's last man out was Spofforth. He had been caught off Barlow, who was England's match-winner with seven wickets for 40 runs, figures marginally better than Spofforth's. Barlow had also done it without his normal studs in his boots because Murdoch had objected to them. The incident began when words were exchanged as Spofforth and George Palmer, Australia's last pair, walked back to the pavilion along with the victorious England team.

While researching his biography of Spofforth, the most thorough Australian academic historian Dr Richard Cashman found several examples of Spofforth's combustible temper. Two occurred on board ship, one on the 1882 trip to England when he insulted a Frenchman and was challenged to a duel. Spofforth had a nervous disposition and a match-winner's ego. He was forever turning down invitations to play, then allowing himself to be persuaded at the last minute, and resenting the popularity accorded to Edwin Evans which Spofforth thought to be his due. It would only have taken a word or two – the wrong word at the wrong time – to wind him up. And Cashman found one contemporary reference to this incident in prose, in the *Age* of 30 January 1883:

> After the match was over an allusion was made in conversation to Spofforth having cut up the wicket with his feet. This so annoyed the demon bowler that he struck out at Mr Read, of the English eleven.

Fortunately for Spofforth, the genial Surrey secretary is as good tempered as he is muscular and contented himself by smiling upon his ill mannered adversary.

There was another contemporary reference, in verse. The *Bulletin*, which brought the bush-verse of Henry Lawson and 'Banjo' Paterson to the Australian public, came out with 'Song of the Spike' in its issue of 3 February 1883:

> 'Twas in the dressing room, and lo,
> When all were gathered round
> Spoff cut up rough on Barlow, 'cause
> He cut up rough the ground . . .
> 'You lie!' cried Barlow, then Spoff 'shaped'
> Quite quick for the affray;
> All thought that spike would cause a great
> *Spiketacular* display.
> Then Read appeared, and said – 'Oh, bosh!
> Of this spike we're all full;
> To fight about a spike is not
> A bit *respiketable.*'
> 'I'll go for you!' then howls out Spoff,
> But Read said – 'No, not quite,
> I come out here for cricket, I
> Did not come out to fight.'

Cashman found another reference to this incident in the *Sydney Sportsman* of 5 January 1916. As it was retold more than thirty years after the event, it is not the most reliable evidence, but it shows that the Spofforth Affair made a lasting impression on somebody's memory: 'One word led to another, and Barlow made some insulting remark to Spofforth and the Demon replied with a blow which knocked Barlow over the seat. A big fight seemed imminent, but friends dragged Spofforth inside, and Walter Read (a champion amateur boxer) stood in front of Barlow to protect him.'

Barlow does not refer to this incident directly in his memoir of this game:

I shall never forget the excitement at the close of this match; it reminded me of the occasion when Australia beat England by seven runs at the Oval in 1882. Our team was vociferously cheered by the great crowd, and most of the gentlemen and myself were called out of the pavilion. When I was coming away for lunch, some of the spectators caught me and carried me shoulder high. I received several presents, including a silver cup; also about £25, which was collected for me on the ground.

Barlow, the model professional, would not stir up a controversy, but he can be seen to refer to this incident by implication in another passage. Bligh's touring party 'was the finest which has ever left England'. The 1886/87 tour, however, was the most enjoyable of his three tours to Australia. Reason? 'The umpiring and other matters incidental to cricket were also much more satisfactory.'

Bligh, of course, made no public reference at any time to this incident but he did in a letter to his father. The England captain, after saying that 'our fellows were very angry' about Spofforth cutting up the wicket, went on: 'We have written a very strong protest to the Sydney committee and to Murdoch telling them that if it occurs again we shall appeal to the umpires.' (Not perhaps the gravest threat ever made in cricket, but in the absence of ICC Match Referees it was about all that an England captain could do.) As for the altercation, Bligh went on:

Spofforth rather nearly came to fisticuffs with Read and Barlow but I think he was excited a little above himself at the time. I only hope there will be no serious row as our trip has been so thoroughly harmonious as yet – the only awkward thing in fact being the very marked comparisons made in the papers between our team and Harris's and W.G.'s in our favour.

So Spofforth 'struck out' at Read. The Demon also aimed 'a blow which knocked Barlow over the seat', and Barlow was only half-fit for the next game in Queensland. 'Rather nearly came to fisticuffs': even Bligh's phrase suggests the antagonists squaring up to each other and perhaps a push here and a shove there. It was the heat of the moment – and it shows that an Ashes Test between

England and Australia in 1883 could become as heated as any Test match since.

*   *   *

England had to sail from Sydney to Brisbane the same afternoon. The fourth day had started early, at 11 a.m., instead of noon, so they could catch the ship and England had the match won by lunchtime. This was a fortunate arrangement as it separated the contestants and allowed tempers to cool.

By inviting English cricketers to the colony for the first time, and entertaining Bligh's men lavishly, Queensland demonstrated it was no longer a backwater. The region had been settled in the 1820s, when it was part of New South Wales, with penal settlements; convicts were then forbidden and only free settlers allowed. In 1859 Queensland became a colony in its own right, although the European population was no more than 20,000, and a parliament was established the following year. Cattle became more numerous than people, gold was discovered, while sugar cane was grown in the north. In 1881, two years before Bligh's visit, the introduction of artesian bore drilling ensured the future of farming in the interior.

Of the fortnight set aside for the visit to Queensland, six days had to be spent on ship, which left time for only two matches, in addition to all the social arrangements. Bligh can almost be seen mopping his brow before writing for *Lillywhite's*: 'We may certainly be said to have reaped one advantage by our enterprise, a reception throughout the time spent there of such universal acclamation as to make it singular, even amidst the bountiful hospitality that was everywhere extended to us.'

His men had to go on a day-trip by train to Toowoomba, engage in two pigeon-shooting matches, watch a corroboree, attend an amateur dramatic performance and a ball. Barlow, who wrote about this leg of the tour for *Athletic News*, wrote of the corroboree in Maryborough, when a huge fire was lit one evening:

The King of the Aborigines was introduced to the Hon Ivo Bligh, and welcomed the latter with a most gracious speech and intensely ceremonial shake of the hand. The next morning the blacks gave us an idea of what they could do in the way of throwing the boomerang – an extraordinary performance, as many of my English friends are no doubt aware.

The first Australian cricket team to tour England, in 1868, had been composed of indigenous Australians. Barlow felt no need to remind his readers of their prowess at throwing the boomerang because their cricket matches had included demonstrations of it.

In Brisbane Bligh's team beat XVIII of Queensland by an innings and 154 runs in two days, not the scheduled three. The English captain summoned up some irony to record:

> At Brisbane the president of the Licensed Victuallers' Assocation honoured the captain with a letter, setting forth the necessity of the English eleven being in their places on the third day (the match being finished in two), for the convincing reason that he had contracted to supply refreshments for three days. This apparently reasonable request an engagement in the country unfortunately prevented us from acceding to.

The game against XVIII of Maryborough was also won by an innings and plenty. It is notable that of the 36 Queensland cricketers in the two games, only one played an innings as high as 20; and only one had a surname that was not British, Voller, who thus augured the German influx which strengthened Queensland cricket. 'There is a lack of good cricketers in Brisbane, and there is a rare opportunity for a competent professional out here' Barlow concluded. 'They wanted one of us to stay, but we could not see leaving Old England. I could do with Queensland well enough if it was not for the excessive heat and the mosquitoes.'

A prize of a plot of land was offered for making the highest score in the game at Maryborough. Read won it, although he sold the plot rather than squatting there. For having been the peacemaker in Sydney, he received his reward in Queensland if not in heaven.

8

Or Not Regained?

England, as a result of going 2-1 up in the Third Test, had regained the Ashes. Or had they?

It is a complicated issue, worthy of lawyers and Queen's Counsels. England, in the form of Bligh's team, had beaten Australia, in the form of Murdoch's team, by two matches to one. But there was still a fourth match to come: between Bligh's team and 'a Combined Eleven'. This was the name to be given to a team chosen from all Australian cricketers, not simply from those contracted to play under Murdoch on their 1882 tour. The difference was small: it meant that Edwin Evans and Frank Allan, a left-arm pace bowler, had become available, but neither was the equal of Spofforth or Palmer so they were change, not opening, bowlers.

It could be argued that it is for history to decide where the goalposts were placed and when; in which case the historians so far have not agreed. Broadly, English cricket historians think England regained the Ashes, 2-1, and Australian cricket historians think Australia retained them, 2-2. The former consider the first three Tests were the basis for judgment; the latter consider the four Tests were. The weight of evidence either way is not conclusive, except for one overwhelming point.

At the time, in the aftermath of the Third Test in Sydney, the general opinion in both hemispheres was that Bligh's men had succeeded in their quest and had regained the ashes of English cricket, not that they had any physical form as yet in the public eye. Some evidence for this opinion is as follows.

During the speeches in the luncheon room at the SCG after the Third Test Bligh said, according to the *Argus*, that:

> When the Australians went home they had beaten the English team, and now the English team had come out here and returned the compliment. Such results were as they should be, merely as interchange of courtesies . . . Mr Murdoch, in responding, expressed regret that as the Eleven was now nearly defunct they would not have another opportunity of meeting their opponents.

Before the Third Test the Australian newspapers had agreed that it was going to be the decisive match of the series, even though a Fourth Test was going to be staged. The day after England had levelled the series at 1-1 in Melbourne, the *Age* had spoken of 'the third and deciding match of the three arranged'; the *Argus* said 'the concluding match remains to be played'; and the *Sydney Morning Herald* called it 'the deciding encounter'.

Murdoch held the same opinion that it was a three-match series, or at least he did up until the Third Test had been lost by Australia. After England had won the Second Test to level the series in Melbourne, the Australian captain said: 'In the match to be played in Sydney in a few days' time we shall strain every nerve to place the final match to the credit of Australia.'

The famous verse from the Melbourne *Punch*, which was to be placed on the urn, was published in the issue of 1 February 1883, after the Third Test. As it celebrates Ivo going 'back with the urn, the urn', the implication again is that the Ashes had been regained in the eyes of the Australian media, if not the public as a whole.

> When Ivo goes back with the urn, the urn;
> Studds, Steel, Read and Tylecote return, return;
> The welkin will ring loud,
> The great crowd will feel proud,
> Seeing Barlow and Bates with the urn, the urn;
> And the rest coming home with the urn.

An affecting, mesmeric verse it is too, far above the doggerel of some contemporary cricket poetry. The old English word 'welkin', meaning the firmament or sky, serves as a natural correlative – the elements roaring approval. The rhyming and the repetition of 'urn' elevate the standard too. Although his offering is all too brief, the anonymous author could claim to come second only to Francis Thompson among cricket poets.

The *Bulletin* in Sydney conceded the series too, as Bligh's players set off for Queensland:

> It's all over, Bligh has gone
> With his ashes, we're forlorn.
> Familiar with us is the sup
> Of the hyssop – bitter cup.

On a date which has been deduced to be 16 February 1883, the eve of the Fourth Test, Ivo Bligh wrote a letter on notepaper supplied by the Australian Club in Sydney, where he and his fellow amateurs were staying. (The letter itself is undated except for 'Friday morning'.) It was written to Mrs Anne Fletcher, a lady from Queensland who had sent him a velvet bag as a present: the famous velvet bag, with the date of 1883 embroidered on it, which can still be seen today. 'My dear Mrs Fletcher' the letter began. 'Many thanks for the pretty little bag you have so kindly sent me. The ashes shall be consigned to it forthwith and always kept there in memory of the great match.' At this point, it is perfectly clear that Bligh believed England had regained the Ashes, whatever happened in the Fourth Test on the morrow.

'Mid-on', the cricket analyst of the *Melbourne Leader*, wrote that Bligh had won the series because the Australian selectors had omitted Harry Boyle from the first three Tests: 'the foolish policy which induced the Australian Eleven Match Committee to discard Boyle thrice, in favour of members of the team whom it was well known were less useful, was alone responsible for Mr Bligh having achieved his highest ambition.' This ambition must have been winning the series and regaining the Ashes.

As correspondent of the *Sportsman*, Cobbett reported after

England had taken the series 2-1: 'Our men thus won the third match and the rubber, and the "Ashes" of which so much was said will come back to England.'

In England, the magazine *Cricket* proclaimed: ' "The revered ashes of English cricket" are by this time on their way to England . . . That they (Bligh's team) should have won the rubber against Murdoch's eleven will be intensely gratifying to English cricketers everywhere.'

Punch, in London, celebrated the news of England's 2-1 victory over Murdoch's Australians by starting a poem, however execrably:

> Hooray! English cricket is still 'all alive oh!'
> We thank you for proving that same, Captain Ivo!

Long after the event, in an issue of the *Cricketer* in 1972, Ralph Barker gave his verdict, as one of the best professional historians to have written in depth about cricket: 'Despite the apparent squaring of the rubber, the verdict of historians has mostly been that the fourth match, although accepted as a Test Match, did not affect the main issue, and today Bligh is remembered as the man who first brought the Ashes back from Australia.'

Another English historian, Rowland Bowen, agreed in *Cricket: A History*:

> . . . the relevance of 'the Ashes' was solely to matches by English teams against Murdoch's 1882 Australians. If this had not been so, if all matches between English and Australian teams were taken into account, the Melbourne ladies would surely not have prepared 'the Ashes' after the third match but would have awaited the fourth match (known for several weeks as a fixture and not hastily arranged after the third – it is from this wrong supposition that so much of the muddle arises).

*   *   *

The goalposts were then shifted. We all know how it happens in various sports in addition to cricket. We agree informally to play a game – perhaps football in the garden – until a stage when one side wins. Then we decide to play on further, until such a score has been reached, but the other side wins.

The Fourth Test was staged in Sydney after the ground-breaking visit to Queensland by Bligh's party. It can be accounted a unique Test match for the number of catches that were dropped and the number of pitches that were used: not one, nor two, but four. It was also far more amicable than the two previous Tests had been. We can conjecture this was because both sides felt the occasion was less intense, and the match less important, than the Ashes-deciding third. The prize was no longer at stake.

After Bligh had won the toss for the third time in a row, Allan Steel played a magnificent innings of 135 not out. 'At starting he shaped as if he would not last long, but upon settling down by-and-by his cutting was hard, clean, and neat, his leg play sound and telling, his driving safe and resolute, and the confidence and vigour wanting in his play at the outset became more and more marked as his performance was drawing to a close' reported the *Australasian*. Steel offered at least three catchable chances that were missed, although that was nothing compared with the number of fielding mistakes he was to make.

In spite of Steel's century, Australia stayed in the game and dismissed England for 263, a total little higher than par for the conditions. Harry Boyle, as predicted by some critics, made a difference by his accuracy, and took five wickets in the match. He was, of course, one of Murdoch's 1882 Australians and therefore could have been selected for the first three Tests. Edwin Evans and the England-born all-rounder William Midwinter were brought in as 'All Australians'. Tom Garrett, Percy McDonnell and – to Bligh's amazement – Hugh Massie were dropped.

Australia reached 262, only 1 run behind, thanks to a fifty from Jack Blackham, who thus emulated Tylecote; to a last wicket stand of 41 between the newcomers Evans and Boyle; and to an astonishing innings of 87 by Bonnor. 'It is to be said that in a lifetime a lover of cricket might never see another similar innings' reported the *Australasian*, who also made the point in mitigation that Bonnor was ill. 'No fewer than one dozen chances, the major portion of them fairly easy ones, can be urged against him, and so it is safe to assert that he had a charmed life. Proverbially a cat has nine lives, and so Bonnor is now able to say that he can give a cat a long start and then come in an easy winner.'

Far and away the main culprit was Steel. The *Australasian* reckoned he missed seven chances, although one 'in the long field' was so difficult that he did not get a hand to it. Bligh in his report for *Lillywhite's* said that Bonnor was missed eight times (one was a missed stumping by Tylecote). In his letter to his father Bligh did not go so far as to repeat his comment that England's catching was 'contemptible', but his vexation can still be sensed between the lines:

> Nat Steel did a great deal to win and almost more to lose the match. He got 135 runs not out, ran out both the Studds badly and missed 5 catches without catching one. Our catching the 2nd day entirely lost us the match. Bonnor was missed 7 or 8 times, most of them easy and early in the innings. There is without doubt something in the atmosphere or light that makes all English elevens very prone to miss catches.

These conditions did not affect George Studd, however, who took four catches. 'The best man in the 22 was undoubtedly G.B. Studd' admitted the *Australasian*, 'and those who witnessed his wonderful dexterity and unceasing brilliance will justly consider his superb exhibition as a criterion by which to gauge all future performance in the field.'

After reading Ivo's letter, and his Bible before anything else that morning, his father might have murmured to himself that whatever Steel had given, Steel had taken away. But there was a very good reason why Steel missed his chances, whether he was at mid-off or at long-off: he was short-sighted. It is amazing that he should have scored two Test hundreds given his eyesight, but at least he must have been able to focus on the ball clearly once it had pitched. In the outfield Steel had little or no chance. Cricketers did not wear spectacles on the field in those days. The first England player who seems to have worn them in an Ashes series was Dick Young, but his two Tests as a wicketkeeper-batsman on the 1907/08 tour of Australia were so ineffective that he too might have been visually handicapped. Teaching maths at Eton was more Young's style.

In their second innings England were dismissed for 197. Spofforth had been at a low ebb in the first innings, perhaps because Evans was playing and thereby hogging his limelight, but he roused himself to bowl Steel and Read. Australia were thus left to make 199 to win. The highest fourth-innings total in the twelve Tests to date had been Australia's 169 for five to win the Second Test at Sydney the previous year, so Australia had to raise the bar appreciably higher. In their favour, however, was the exceptional circumstance that each side had a different pitch for each innings in this Test. Before they started their fourth-innings chase, the Australians went out and bowled on several pitches before deciding which one was best suited to their batsmen. They made everything they could of the advantage which was legitimately offered to them, but it seems to have been an experiment that was never repeated in Test cricket again. England bowled the enormous number of 163.1 four-ball overs in Australia's second innings but the hosts crossed the line in the end, thanks to Blackham becoming the first wicketkeeper to score two fifties in a Test. The only man to have played in every Test to date was met with an ovation and carried into the pavilion by his friends.

Australia had thus levelled the rubber at 2-2, and the debate was re-opened: had England regained the Ashes by two Tests to one, or had Australia now retained them? Immediately, too, the question was raised as to whether a fifth Test could now be played, to determine the outcome plainly. Melbourne was to stage the last first-class game of Bligh's tour, a return match against Victoria in March, and this could easily have been converted into a fifth Test. In his letter home to his father on 28 February Bligh reported without any need for restraint: 'We are only going to play one more match, either v the combined team [i.e. Australia] or Victoria. As usual the 2 colonies or rather the cricket authorities in them are fighting tooth and nail as to which it is to be.'

No agreement was reached between the associations of NSW and

Victoria. So Bligh's team continued with their original schedule and played Victoria in a de-mob spirit in their final match, losing by an innings. (In *Lillywhite's* Bligh confesses that after the Fourth Test in Sydney, and upon hearing there was to be no fifth Test, his players gave themselves over to other pursuits, such as lawn tennis.) The issue of the Ashes was not going to be resolved on the field of play and therefore had to be discussed in the newspapers, speeches, and general conversation.

From the outset of Bligh's tour it had always been intended that his team would play one match against a team drawn from all Australian cricketers: an 'additional' match against a combined XI, it was usually called. Certainly, after losing the First Test, Bligh told his father in a letter home that he and his team had three more matches to come against Australia. To this debate it is not relevant at what stage this fourth match was finalised, whether before or during the tour; its status does. Did England's schedule consist of a three-match series against the 1882 Australians for the Ashes, plus an additional match against a combined XI; or a four-Test series for the Ashes?

The evidence for the latter is less plentiful. Whereas all Australian and English authorities agreed after the Third Test that England had won the Ashes, after the Fourth Test it was only Australian authorities who thought the home side had retained them – plus support from one English source, Cobbett. After Australia had levelled the series at 2-2 in Sydney, the *Sportsman* proclaimed: 'They have . . . prevented the return of the "Ashes" to the mother country.'

Perhaps the most interesting, and authoritative, verdicts came at the farewell dinner at the end of the tour. It was given by the Melbourne Cricket Club on 13 March 1883, Bligh's 24th birthday, and was held in their pavilion, bedecked with flags and banners saying 'au revoir'. Sir William Clarke was absent but the somewhat portentous vice-president F.G. Smith was present to give the audience of eighty gentlemen the benefit of his long-windedness. This occasion was the equivalent of the award presentations on television at the end of a modern Test series.

Before tackling the question of the Ashes, Smith said the tourists were 'the pleasantest of pleasant men', which prompted applause from the guests. The committee, he said, felt under the deepest obligations to Mr Bligh for the alacrity with which he had adopted all their plans, and for the immense assistance which he had rendered throughout their difficult, and it might be said, now that it was drawing to a close, successful enterprise. (Yes, a successful enterprise, and not merely financially.) Smith then asked all present to join him in congratulating Mr Bligh on achieving his highest ambition in Australia, namely, the recovery of what had been humorously termed the 'revered ashes of English cricket'. The newspaper reports of this speech mention the reaction of the guests to these words as 'Applause'. They also say that in the course of the evening some guests shouted 'no'. On this occasion they did not – which suggests that some sections at least of informed Australian opinion still thought England had regained the Ashes.

Bligh had to reply to this speech, and he did so in a light-hearted, witty vein, which prompted plenty of laughter as well as applause; but his reply was not without some ambiguity. Firstly, though, came the serious point that he and his players had found out only a fortnight before, after the Fourth Test, what had been ailing Fred Morley during their tour: in the collision which the *Peshawur* had with the *Glenroy* on the voyage out to Australia, Morley had broken one of his ribs. Not until 27 February had a doctor diagnosed it properly. (In a letter home Bligh told his father: 'No wonder the poor fellow has been unable to bowl, field or do anything else. He had been treated previously by several doctors all of whom failed to find this out.') Loud applause greeted Bligh when he said everyone now admired Morley's pluck for playing as much as he had with such a wound.

The English captain then tackled the issue of the Ashes. Confrontational by nature he was not. In fact in the same letter home that he mentioned Morley's injury, he admitted to his father that his team were not altogether happy with his diplomatic approach to the incident of the studs in Sydney ('a good many of our fellows declared that I was much to [sic] easy with them in giving in on certain points'). Now Bligh was firm in his self-effacing manner. He was not going to allow Murdoch, his counterpart, to take the glory.

The summary of the central part of Bligh's speech is important enough to reproduce as it was published in the newspapers, in this case the *Argus*. Bligh referred to his first speech to the MCC members on his team's arrival in Melbourne, when he said they had come to beard the lion or kangaroo in his den:

Now that four months had passed, he was afraid that the kangaroo hopped as jauntily as ever (laughter). He was afraid that it must be confessed, also, with regard to those 'ashes' referred to by the chairman, that the team could not take them back to England. The best thing to do with them would be for their respected friend Mac [curator or groundsman at the MCG] to bury them in some corner of the ground (loud laughter and applause). There was only one thing he had to request, and that was that all present would see to it that none of Murdoch's eleven touched them, because they really had no right to them (laughter and applause).

Of the several points Bligh made here, the most significant is that he and his team could not take the Ashes back to England – but that none of Murdoch's players had the right to touch them either. On the surface this suggests that Bligh reckoned the result of the series – two-all – was significant, but equally so was the fact that Murdoch's 1882 Australians lost 2-1. On this public occasion, dominated by bonhomie, Bligh at his most diplomatic did not say that England had won or lost the series, regained or not regained the Ashes. In the spirit of 'After you, Claude', he said that both sides had done awfully well and cricket was the winner. Mr Smith had said that England had regained the Ashes, but Bligh modestly refused this accolade. Bligh took the debate forwards, but not by much, and neither in his letters home nor in his report on the tour for *Lillywhite's* did he clarify which side held the Ashes.

When the magazine *Cricket* reviewed Bligh's tour, its editorial – presumably written by Charles Alcock – was also ambivalent.

We have heard much about the 'revered ashes of English cricket' in connection with this tour, but it is not our intention in any way to touch on the question of the present resting place of those interesting relics. The English Captain quaintly suggested the advisability of a decent burial, and no one on this side will, we fancy, object to their interment. The team which the Hon Ivo Bligh commanded have done very much to uphold the reputation of English cricketers . . .

Perhaps the most balanced judgment came from Melbourne in the pages of the *Argus*.

As regards the result of the tour in a purely cricketing sense, the honours are once more evenly divided. The avowed object of the visit was to wrest, if possible, from Murdoch's victorious Australian team the title of supremacy in the cricket-field which on Kennington Oval they had just won from a representative eleven of England. A series of matches with Murdoch's team was made the primal condition of the tour, and as far as this ruling object is concerned the Hon Ivo Bligh and his companions can in the future look back with a feeling of pride on this particular portion of their expedition. Three matches were played. In all of them the verdict was unmistakeable, and at the end the balance of power rested with the English team.

The commentary went on to deplore the wet weather which had afflicted the three Tests, then concluded: 'No absolute and final settlement of the question of supremacy as between the best teams of England and Australia was involved in the contest, for the solution of this interesting problem will no doubt be frequently attempted both on English and Australian cricket grounds within the next decade.' The primal condition, however, the three-Test series, had ended in England's favour.

More conclusive than anything that anybody said, Bligh included, was what Bligh did. He was polite and self-effacing in his speeches. But he was given possession of the actual urn, by some Australian women, and he took the urn home. If possession is nine-tenths of the law, Bligh regained the Ashes.

For half a century *Wisden Cricketers' Almanack* has declared that the urn was presented to Bligh after England had won the Third Test in Sydney. So it was, but surely not by some Australian ladies in Sydney, as *Wisden* implies, but by the ladies of Rupertswood – the ones he spent every spare moment with, the ones who went to the

MCG to cheer for him, if not for England. When interviewed by the *Cricket Field* magazine in 1894, only eleven years after the event, Bligh recounted how he and his players had set out to regain the Ashes, after the Oval defeat in 1882: 'and when we had beaten Murdoch's team the second time a number of Australian ladies presented me with a pretty little urn containing ashes, which, according to the title written on the urn, were "The ashes of English cricket." I still keep this as one of my most cherished possessions.'

The original ashes had been burned on Christmas Eve, after the social match in the paddock involving the eight English amateurs. The contents may then have been updated, in that one of the bails used in the Third Test at Sydney may have been burned to ashes. A supporting piece of evidence for this is that another bail from the Third Test was turned into the handle of a paper-knife which the Clarke family used at Rupertswood. It is reasonable to suppose that one of the England amateurs took a pair of bails from the stumps after the Third Test as a memento. (Barlow was renowned as a collector of memorabilia but at the time he had his hands full with Spofforth.) The bails may then have been given to the Clarkes before the end of the tour, one of them going into the paper-knife, the other into the urn.

The urn may have been updated too. If it had originally been wooden, it was now replaced by the present terracotta urn. MCC's assistant librarian Glenys Williams is convinced that the urn – the present one – came from one of the dressing-tables used by the ladies at Rupertswood. There it would have been used for holding perfumes or make-up or the like.

Ashes and urn were then placed in the velvet bag which Mrs Fletcher had given to Bligh. There is no reason to disbelieve the written pledge by the England captain that they would be 'consigned forthwith' to the velvet bag. Bligh had done what he had set out to do. He had gone to Australia to recover the metaphorical ashes of the body of English cricket, and he had been presented with a real urn containing ashes to embody the feat. Bligh took the Ashes home, put them on his mantelpiece, and nobody in his lifetime argued that they were not his to keep.

Well, that is not strictly the case. After Victoria had beaten Bligh's team in the final match of their tour, the Ashes were claimed for Victoria (disregarding the fact that the English XI had beaten the colony by ten wickets in the first of their two matches). A humorous booklet by R.D. Beeston came out later in 1883 entitled 'St Ivo and The Ashes. A Correct, True and Particulat History of the Hon Ivo Bligh's Crusade in Australia.' The fact that it was published in Melbourne can be deduced by the following comment about the England team's reaction to their innings defeat by Victoria:

> In the dead of night, in a secluded corner of the MCC ground, the lion mournfully buried the ashes, a few kangaroos looking sympathisingly on. The headstone of the tomb is shaped from a broken bat, on which is the following inscription:
>
>
>
> CI GIT*
> The Sacred Ashes,
> Awaiting
> For a Time
> The Regaining of Supremacy
> By
> English Cricket.
>
>
>
> N.B. – None of Murdoch's Eleven need apply.

In this parochial view, too, Australia had not won the Ashes. Victoria had.

*   *   *

Bligh's mission in Australia, however, had not been fully accomplished. The telegram, in response to his letter asking his father and mother for permission to marry, had arrived. His parents had not granted it. What the exact words of the telegram were, Bligh does not tell us either in his letters or diary, but it is manifest that his parents had not responded in the affirmative.

'I got your telegram all right and it is about that I am principally

*Old French for 'Here lie/s'.

anxious to write to you' Bligh wrote in his wide-ranging letter home of 28 February 1883. 'It was rather what I suspected, naturally under the circumstances. But even though I cannot get your letter sent to Auckland for some time yet containing an explanation I am going to ask you to consider the circumstances again.' Was the parental response an outright no? Or did they advise waiting until their son had returned home to Cobham Hall and given them a full account, which would have entailed a cooling-off period for his passion?

'I will tell you one of my great reasons for doing so' Bligh went on, to explain why he wanted his parents to reconsider their decision.

> When we left Queensland a report got about in Melbourne and was actually posted up at the newspaper offices and all over the town that we were all drowned and the steamer lost. Most unfortunately this was carried direct to my dear Florrie's ears and the consequence of the shock has been that she was very seriously ill for some days. She fainted twice that day and then for 3 days had incessant returns of the same attacks leaving her weaker each time. Thank God she is now much better, well on the road to recovery. Well you can imagine father how terribly unwilling this has made me to leave her right the other end of the world probably for some months. The dear girl is of course very very anxious that I should not leave her but like the true hearted girl that she is says if it is really right for me to go she would advise me to do so.

Bligh had intended to visit New Zealand on the way home, along with the two Georges, Studd and Vernon. In the letter he tells his father that he will instead stay in Australia, and have his father's letter redirected from Auckland to Melbourne. He goes on, with a growing hint of desperation, to oppose what was obviously his parents' demand that he should return to Kent before doing anything precipitate:

> I do hope you will re-consider things. Think what a terrible thing it is to have to leave my poor girl all that time – still worse that awful distance away, as far apart as we could possibly be in the world! Put yourself under the same circumstances and father I think you will

well understand my great anxiety. You see it really wd not make much difference whether I was married and brought Florrie home with me or came out again in a few months. I have told you in other letters how that even had I to come out here and work as a clerk I would do so willingly sooner than lose Florrie – and is it worth while that we should both have the pain of such a separation in order that I might come home and discuss my prospects etc. We would both be content to live in the very quietest way – even if you thought I had better wait till you could see what had better be done I would wait out here. At any rate whatever happens I shall wait till I get an answering telegram to this. The Clarkes would manage everything in connection with the wedding as they have just done with Lord Charles Scott and Miss Ryan. We were all up there and the ceremony went off capitally. I have been up there a good deal lately and go up again tomorrow as Florrie has been there all the while. Dear me – I do so wish you and mother could but see Florrie for half an hour. I am sure you would both love her very much for she is such a really noble-hearted girl. I have made acquaintance lately with a good number of her friends and it is no exaggeration to say that she is the favourite of half the nicest people in Melbourne.

Bligh's parents had not slammed shut the door against his marriage to Florence Morphy. They had not opened it either. Maybe the phrase 'cut you off without a penny' had been used in the telegram, but probably not. It would have been too expensive for a start. The telegraph from England to Australia had been opened in 1872, and a telegram cost a minimum of ten pounds.

24. According to his slightly condescending profile in *Vanity Fair*: 'Mr Spofforth is Australian by origin and breeding, yet, like all the better kind of Australians, he is not distinguishable from an English gentleman.' This was written on his first tour of England in 1878. Later opinion of the Demon might not have been so effusive.

26. The Studd brothers, who captained Cambridge University in three consecutive seasons from 1882. From the left: Kynaston (the eldest), Charles and George. Kynaston, who was later knighted, led a more worldly existence than the other two, founding the London Polytechnic and becoming Lord Mayor of London in 1928.

25. The Hon. Alfred Lyttelton. According to his profile in *Vanity Fair* : 'By profession he is a barrister, and, as such, is second "Devil" to the present Attorney-General, who honours him with especial confidence.' This appeared in 1884, when Lyttelton took off his wicketkeeping gloves during the Oval Test and took four Australian wickets for 14 with lobs.

27. According to his teammate George Giffen, George Bonnor was 'one of the finest specimens of manhood. When, exerting all the strength in that Herculean frame, he smote the bowling, it was a sight for the gods.'

28. Frederick Spofforth in 1882, his prime. The eyes capture some of the demonic intensity.

29. George Bonnor, according to *Vanity Fair*'s profile, was 'a most excellent specimen of the Greater Briton'. Aside from his fame as a hitter, they noted that Bonnor could also 'bowl very fast indeed'. Yet he bowled very little and took only 12 first-class wickets.

30. The Victorian side that defeated England at the end of Bligh's tour. Probable identities: Back row: Elliot (ump), Scott, Turner, Blackham, Hope (ump), McShane. Front row: Boyle, Midwinter, Bonnor, Cooper, Horan, Palmer, McDonnell. Only Turner never played in Tests.

31. The Melbourne Cricket Ground in 1877 at the time of the first-ever Test. Left to right: the scorers' box, the press box and members' grandstand. The trees in the background were considered by Bligh's team to make catching difficult.

33. Ivo's elder brother, Edward, Lord Clifton, in his twenties. He became the Seventh Earl of Darnley. He was still bowling fast for Kent between bouts of mental instability.

32. According to Ivo's profile in *Vanity Fair* in 1904; 'he is an all round sportsman, as well as a man of manners … He has been president of the M.C.C.; but he has now descended to golf.' The original cartoon sold for more than £20,000.

34. Cobham Hall around the time Ivo inherited. The magnificent carved stone coat of arms high above the central door blew down in a gale after the Second World War.

35. Ivo around the time he became Earl of Darnley in 1900.

36. Ivo shooting on the Cobham estate before the First World War. The Game Book for 24 Dec 1906: 'Four guns (Ld Darnley, Henry Bligh, Clifton and Noel Bligh): 12 pheasant cocks, 18 pheasant hens, 1 woodcock, 11 mallard, 1 wood pigeon, 3 hares and two rabbits – Total 48.'

37. The Library at Cobham Hall in 1901. Tradition has it that the Ashes were kept on the mantelpiece. While the Fourth Earl's portrait still hangs above the fire, the fine furniture has been carried off by 'the enemy', Clifton's widow Jemima, and replaced by Edwardian sundries.

38. A British Airship flying low over Cobham Hall during the First World War.

39. Darnley, tall as ever, on the steps of Cobham Hall shortly before the First World War.

40. Ivo's second son, Noel, a Rifle Brigade man, married three times and became a landscape artist. His daughter Jasmine, by his first marriage, was the first woman announcer when the B.B.C. opened its regular television service. She too was married three times, finally to Howard Marshall, the famous radio Test commentator.

41. Ivo and Florence outside the Gilt Hall surrounded by Australian servicemen during the First World War when Cobham Hall served as a hospital. Florence, revelling in her 'Mother Bountiful' role, received a D.B.E. in 1919 for her services. Ivo, now wearing a white beard, was said to have been aged by the experience.

43. A portrait of Ivo in the last decade of his life, which bears out *Vanity Fair*'s summary: 'an unassuming, upright, very popular fellow with a very gentle voice'.

42. Florence and her daughter Dorothy in early happy years before becoming Countess. On her only return voyage, in 1903–4, she and Dorothy travelled on board the S.S. *Orontes*, the same ship as Plum Warner's M.C.C. team.

44. The main entrance arch to Cobham Hall, above which used to sit a collection of cannons.

45. The Coming of Age of Ivo and Florence's eldest son Clifton, seated between his parents. All the family are present, including Uncle Arthur, Ivo's younger brother, who is standing far right. He brought back from Paris both a French beard and a large collection of erotica.

46. Ivo as the doting grand-parent with Tony Peploe, the co-author's father.

47. Ivo's daughter Dorothy or 'Dolly'. Six foot tall but not the beauty her mother had hoped for; their relationship broke down in later years when Florence developed Alzheimer's. When told her mother was dying she is supposed to have said 'I haven't seen the old dragon for ten years, why bother now?

9

The Second Quest

No victory parade was held in Trafalgar Square, no reception at No 10 Downing Street, for the English cricketers on their return to England, as if they had been Sir Garnet Wolseley. For one thing, they did not return as a group but in dribs and drabs. The four professionals set sail from Melbourne first, as they had work to do in the home season of 1883. The amateurs split into those who went back westwards, by the route they had come, like Charles Studd, who had to captain Cambridge University, and those who headed east to New Zealand and North America before reaching home in mid-summer. George Studd, in the latter party, visited Los Angeles where he was to spend the last half-century of his life.

Bligh had intended to go with the second party to New Zealand for some sightseeing and on to America, but urgent business decreed otherwise. He had to hasten home, not to play cricket for Kent, but to see his parents and ask their permission to marry Florence. He departed Melbourne with the grateful thanks of the Melbourne Cricket Club, for the visit had not only been a triumph of diplomacy but a lucrative venture which had enriched the club by several thousand pounds. Bligh boarded the SS *Rosetta*, where he was quartered in a forward cabin which corresponded exactly to his cabin on the *Peshawur*. He wrote a letter to his father two days out from Colombo in which he said that he expected to see the wreckage of the *Glenroy* – 'our old enemy' – in Colombo harbour. He added that he expected to reach Plymouth on 26 May 1883, and would 'bolt up to London as hard as I can and try to be in time for the University Match.'

Although he did not know it at the time of his voyage, Bligh was returning home to something of a hero's welcome and at least one rave review. Australia, more than most colonies, had become a magnet for second and third sons of the gentry and well-to-do. It was a place where they could go and make their fortune, perhaps by exploring and discovering the great inland sea which was thought to exist. As the second son of a relatively poor aristocrat, Bligh too had no inheritance lined up and had to make his own way in the world. And how handsomely, how gallantly, he had done it so far!

On 16 March 1883, the magazine *Cricket – Weekly Record of the Game* launched a new series on its front page. Who else could be the subject of the first profile than the English captain in Australia?

> At the present time it would be difficult to name an English sportsman of any kind more deservedly popular than the Hon Ivo Francis Walter Bligh. Just now indeed there could hardly be a more fitting subject for the inauguration of a gallery of cricket notables than the Captain of the team starting on their homeward journey after so worthily upholding the honour of the Old Country in the Australian Colonies.

For company on the voyage home Bligh had none of his teammates – just a chum in Morton Lucas, an old Harrovian who had been visiting Australia and played a little for Sussex, and his wife, who had 'struck up a tremendous friendship with Florrie'. This time no tea was dispensed on deck at 4 p.m. by Janet Clarke, as he had fondly recounted in his poem. But Bligh was no longer in such need of tea and sympathy, because he was no longer searching so earnestly. The Studd brothers were still searching, but Bligh had found what he had been looking for in large part, a woman's warmth. 'It was terrible hard work parting with her, poor girl' he wrote to his father. 'She was very much cut up but she knows now that nothing but time can separate us.'

After an uneventful voyage, by comparison with the journey out, Bligh went home to Cobham Hall to speak to his parents and urge his case. We do not know which route he took from Plymouth and London but if he arrived back at the nearest railway station to

Cobham Hall, Sole Street, he had the choice of going by foot or horse-drawn vehicle up the main drive to the Hall. In size and spaciousness his family home must have reminded him of Rupertswood on the other side of the world; and Cobham Hall too had its own cricket ground. The Englishness of the setting, however, outweighed similarities with the Antipodes. On the northern edge of the park runs the Roman road of Watling Street. Close by is the Pilgrims' Way from London to Canterbury Cathedral.

Bligh would have first caught sight of a pink turret through the trees of Cobham Park, a couple of square miles in area, with the estate farms beyond. Nothing ostentatious about Cobham Hall: it has a diffidence, a reticence, in the character of the Darnley family. No massive lodge proclaims the entrance to the main drive. There is another entrance, to Lime Avenue, a line of trees which runs for a thousand yards up to the Hall, but the Avenue was used only for family funerals and its entrance was merely a wooden gate. Charles Dickens was given keys to the park and it became his favourite place to relax: he took his last walk there before he died. The deer which roamed through the park had to be shot occasionally but were never hunted. The Darnleys abominated hunting as much as Oscar Wilde ('the unspeakable in pursuit of the uneatable'). They were Whigs by nature, not Tories. They were Irish and Scots in background, not Norman.

The first known Bligh to make a mark was John Bligh, Member of Parliament for Athboy in County Meath where he had a large estate. The famous satirist Jonathan Swift called him 'a puppy of a figure, with a fine Chariot'. Yet in 1713 this Irish puppy succeeded in marrying a first cousin of Queen Anne. One of the most eligible maidens of the early eighteenth century, Lady Theodosia Hyde, not only owned Cobham Hall but was also one of the few Englishwomen to be a peeress in her own right.

Lady Hyde was a descendant of the Royal House of Stuart. Her great aunt had been 'La Belle Stuart' at the court of King Charles II after his restoration in 1680. The King had fallen head over heels for this beauty, although it is not certain whether she became his mistress. At his royal command, Frances Stuart became the model for Britannia, so that her image endured on the reverse side of the British copper coinage until recently.

While Frances Stuart lived at Cobham Hall from 1667 to 1677, a major change to the building was made. Originally the Hall consisted of two long Tudor wings built between 1584 and 1602 and renowned for their fireplaces, which were commissioned by the Lord Cobham of the day from a Flemish craftsman. 'La Belle Stuart' had these two parallel wings joined by a central block to form a capital H. Of this new cross-piece, the masterpiece was the Gilt Hall, which needed 12,000 leaves of gold to decorate the ceiling. This Hall, two storeys in height, not completed until the 1790s, earned the accolade from the Prince Regent of being the 'finest room in all Europe'.

Other features of Cobham Hall came to include a red granite sarcophagus in the shape of a bath, brought back from Italy by the Fourth Earl of Darnley even though it was ten feet long and weighed six tons; and several paintings by Rubens in the East Wing and by Titian in the West, not mere copies as there were at Rupertswood. The main painting in the Gilt Hall was the enormous portrait by Van Dyke of the ill-fated brothers Lord Bernard and Lord John Stuart, sons of the Duke of Lennox, who were killed in the royal cause during the Civil War. It was to be Bligh's unhappy task to sell this painting in the 1920s. It later graced Lord Mountbatten's dining room at Broadlands before ending up in London at the National Portrait Gallery. Gainsboroughs and Reynolds and Flemish tapestries filled the gaps on the walls, while Chippendale furniture competed for space with collections of Dresden.

The Fourth Earl, besides spending lots of money on collecting, was an all-round sportsman. He was one of the pioneers of yacht racing as he took his own cutter to Cowes and other regattas. One of the earliest matches recorded in *Scores and Biographies* is of the match at Lord's between Kent, captained by the Fourth Earl of Darnley, and Hampshire, led by the Earl of Winchilsea. The *History of Kent County Cricket Club*, edited by Lord Harris, records that the Fourth Earl played nine matches for the county between 1790 and 1796. His brother, Honourable Edward Bligh, who became a general, claimed not to have a finger which had not been broken at cricket (he scorned the use of gloves).

The Fifth Earl of Darnley was far more frugal than his father, which was just as well as much of the family wealth had been spent. He was 'low church', and his wife Emma Parnell lower still, so that the children were brought up in an austere milieu amid warnings of Hell's fire. He took a first in Classics, which not many peers did; and he revived the cricket ground at Cobham Hall during his short time as Earl, between 1831 and 1835. Family letters show that he had a melancholy nature and was racked with worries about his wealth and health. He became convinced he was going to die young; and one day he went for a walk in the park, saw some estate workers cutting a tree, and decided to show them the best way to cut a root in half. The axe he wielded glanced off the root, struck his left foot, and within a day or two lockjaw had set in. He left an eight-year-old son, Edward, who was to become Ivo's father. Two other sons became clergymen and played cricket for Kent.

Seldom, even in Victorian England, can a child have been brought up in more repressed circumstances than Edward, the Sixth Earl of Darnley. His father had gone, but not the austerity. His widowed mother excelled herself by quoting such happy passages from the Bible as 'he that spareth the rod hateth the child', and called upon the butler to apply the birch unceasingly on her infant children. A lifelong devotion to religion was instilled, and emotional repression. Edward took himself so seriously that, before he came of age, he wrote to all the members of his family to request that in future they should address him as 'Darnley'. He was a stickler for etiquette, perhaps because he felt so shy and inhibited behind the façade. He was a generous host, though, whether at his own cricket ground at Cobham, or at Canterbury when he was President of Kent County Cricket Club, or at Lord's, when he was President of MCC. On his voyage home from Australia Bligh must have fancied his chances of winning his father over to the idea of Florence as a daughter-in-law, because underneath the gruff paternal exterior some humanity had survived intact.

Bligh's mother, Harriet, the eldest daughter of the Earl of

Chichester, 'stiff as a ramrod and as frigid as a glacier', was also not quite so austere as she seemed, at least by the time she mellowed in middle age. Bligh might not have known it by the time he came home to seek parental permission, but she was exceedingly shy and on grand occasions, when the Gilt Hall and the state rooms were alive and bustling, she wanted to melt into the wallpaper rather than discharge her duties as hostess. Her letters show that she had a whimsical humour. She had great affection for her children – even her first son, Lord Clifton, in spite of his psychological problems – and for her grandchildren. Like her husband, and many upper-class Victorians, she was less inhibited with the written word than the spoken.

The great debate seems to have taken six weeks, from the end of May 1883 until mid-July, and we do not know whether the Hall resounded with arguments, tears and slammed doors, and whispering among the servants. The Sixth Earl and his wife must have been alarmed at the thought of their second son marrying a poor governess. If they had been in favour, they would have telegraphed their approval and allowed Bligh to marry Florence in Australia instead of returning home. At least there was a pleasant setting for the debate. We can imagine father and son walking through the park, discussing the prospects for the shooting season, and other sport, before bringing themselves to broach the subject of his burning passion. If they did not care to walk down Lime Avenue, they could stroll to the miniature Stonehenge which the Third Earl had made in the grounds; or to the Swiss Chalet, which had been given to Dickens and which had been presented on the novelist's death to Bligh's father.

Eventually came the puff of smoke in the form of a letter from the Sixth Earl of Darnley, of Cobham Hall, Gravesend, to Miss Florence Morphy on 11 July 1883. It was written in a large, if not generous hand:

> Dear Miss Morphy
>   It is by Ivo's authority and at his instance that I take the liberty of introducing myself to you, so far as this can be done by means of pen, ink and paper.

We were of course much delighted to see him at home once more, looking so much better than was the case when he went out, with but one subject of anxiety. As to this, I can assure you that you and Ivo have the best wishes of Lady Darnley and myself, for although we have never had the pleasure of seeing you, we have otherwise had ample means of satisfying ourselves that we should be able cordially to welcome you as a relation.

You will have no doubt learned from Ivo that it is not exactly an easy matter to me to give him a start in life and there has been a disappointment as to one opening which had appeared to present itself, and we have not as yet been able to do anything definite in another direction, but we have hopes – although the most I can do for him will be small in comparison to what I could wish – I must now say good bye, and with kind regards. I remain, yours very sincerely

Darnley

Not exactly effusive. Not stiff and unbending either. By the standards of his time, and his class, perhaps Darnley's overture could be rated mildly warm.

*   *   *

The wedding, as so often, was easier than the marriage. The Clarkes, as Bligh had suggested they would, arranged everything 'capitally' at Rupertswood. Well, almost everything. Bligh had to find a ring and a best man. When he returned to Australia, he bought a ruby, as well as a diamond engagement ring. For best man, on 11 February 1884 at St Mary's Church in Sunbury, he intended to have George Vernon, but the double international could not face giving a long speech to the august audience of 200 guests who had been brought by special train from Melbourne. Vernon could do no more than respond to the toast to the health of Bligh's cricket team-mates.

In the week before the wedding, *Punch* in Melbourne anticipated one of the social highlights of the season. Bligh might have winced when, once again, his school nickname of Nellie was invoked. Or maybe, now that he was about to marry a younger but stronger woman, he felt secure enough to take it all in good part. The ditty was entitled 'England v Australia – another "Match"', to the air 'Nelly Bligh', and is just about witty enough to reproduce in full:

> Ivo Bligh
> Heaved a sigh
> When across the main,
> Said – 'Unto Victoria's shores
> I'll go back again.'
> Hi Ivo! Ho Ivo!
> Cupid takes a turn,
> Puts to Ivo's heart his torch,
> And 'Ivo's ashes' burn.
> Ivo Bligh's
> Roguish eyes
> Make a sudden 'catch',
> Sees a Southern beauty here,
> And seeks to play a 'match'.
> Hi Ivo! Ho Ivo!
> The Phoenix is the same,
> From his 'ashes' he will rise
> To play the same old game.
> Ivo Bligh
> Means to try
> A life of married bliss.
> Let's hope that it will be a 'hit',
> Although he seeks a 'miss'.
> Hi Ivo! Ho Ivo!
> Happy may you be!
> May bad luck never 'run you out'
> From your felicity.
> Ivo Bligh
> Need not cry
> For cricket's ashes more,
> Since he takes his flame away
> To burn on England's shore.
> Hi Ivo! Ho Ivo!
> This truth never doubt –
> A married man is best 'at home'
> And should be seldom 'out'.

At 1.30 p.m. on the day itself Miss Morphy entered the church on the arm of Sir William Clarke, who gave her away (Janet was one of the choristers). The bride wore a brocaded white silk dress trimmed with Honiton lace. The veil was fastened with a diamond arrow given to her by the bridegroom. The eight bridesmaids wore Cambridge blue, a thoughtful touch. Their baskets of flowers were of cerise and yellow as a compliment to the colours of Bligh and his cricket team. At the wedding breakfast in the ballroom at Rupertswood Lord William Neville gave the best man's speech which Vernon had avoided.

According to the Melbourne *Argus*, Bligh in his reply to the toast of the day said that it had always been easier to make a speech after his team had played a winning match, and the same applied this morning. Then all too soon, in early afternoon, the couple left to spend their wedding night at the residence of Sir George Verdon at Macedon, while the other guests dined, danced and partied until the special train took them back to Melbourne at 10.30 p.m. It was an omen, and not a happy one. While his friends lived life to the full, as his new wife was no doubt ready to do too, Ivo did not have the vitality to join in. Giving speeches, we know from his previous letters, left him feeling 'all knocked up' the following day, and it was no exception at his wedding. The mordant preoccupation with health of the Fifth Earl of Darnley, who had died prematurely as he himself had foreseen, had been inherited by the Sixth Earl, and by his son Ivo too. The Blighs of Cobham Hall enjoyed all the advantages that anyone could have, but a pronounced neurotic tendancy was more often than not their Achilles heel. Ivo, in full measure, had inherited the family characteristic of hypochondria.

During his glittering youth the illness had not surfaced. He was kept busy at school at Cheam and Eton with his sports and studies. It did not surface either during his first three years at Cambridge: by his third season, 1880, he was at the top of his game in cricket as in other sports, opening the batting in the Varsity Match and setting up Cambridge's victory by top-scoring. Off the field too he was enjoying life as president of the amateur dramatic club at Cambridge. In 1881 the problem appeared in earnest when, although he was the university captain, he missed most of the season. 'I was very ill all through the term and if I made about 15 runs I felt quite done up' Bligh was to recall in later life. 'I gave up fielding deep and used to stand at point, which I thought was a much less interesting position. But this was perhaps only because I was unable to enjoy fielding at all.'

In 1882 Bligh did not play a single first-class match while organising the tour to Australia. The reason given was 'ill health', nothing more specific than that. In his diary and letters he offers various causes for his other indispositions. First was the right hand he cut while engaged in tug-of-war on the *Peshawur*, which was real enough, even if it seemed to take an uncommonly long time to heal. Second was lumbago, which prevented him fielding on the second day of the Second Test in Melbourne. Then he had jaundice; then he had liver trouble; then it was digestive organs in general which were playing up; then dyspepsia, both for himself and Florence once they were married. It sounds laughable, a fit young athlete in the prime of life obsessing about being 'all knocked up' after a dance or a speech, but the illness, whether imaginary or not in its origin, became real. By the late 1880s, when in his own late 20s, he was down to ten stone, not the correct weight for a man of 6ft 3in. A modern doctor might diagnose Ivo Bligh as having myalgic encephalomyelitis (ME).

He was happy enough during the honeymoon in New Zealand in March 1884. He wrote to his father from Lake Wakatipu:

> We have got over to New Zealand all safely as you will see from the above address and are staying at a really very pretty place called Queenstown on the shores of the largest lake in New Zealand (I think). Today we had a very pleasant drive up about 15 miles to another small town – Arrowtown – the drive being through some very steep passes between the mountains. Florrie has never seen snow before and is delighted with the scenery.

Florence had much more energy than her husband. From her earliest travels she collected specimens of local flora and inserted them into her diaries or letters. So diverse is the collection from habitats around the world which she assembled at Cobham Hall that Kew Gardens are hoping to propagate some of the rarer seeds.

The new couple arrived together in England in the summer of 1884. In August of that year *Baily's Magazine* welcomed Bligh home with a portrait of this celebrity sportsman. 'Few have been more deadly with the bat and the racquet' *Baily's* proclaimed. 'Independently of his big advantages of height and reach, his performance in all sports has been conspicuous for admirable coolness and judgment.' The magazine anticipated his return to the cricket field; still only 25, he had so much to give to Kent and, if he could regain his form of 1880, and work on his defensive technique, to England too. More than any previous captain of England, Bligh had brought amateur and professional together and united them. Had he played on as England's captain, would he have had amateurs and professionals changing in the same dressing-room half a century before they did? Would Ranjitsinhji have had to wait to make his England debut until the Second Test of 1896 (when he became the first Test batsman to score a century before lunch)? MCC had refused to select an Indian for the First Test, no matter that he was a Cambridge Blue and the outstanding talent of his generation. But the England captain who first regained the Ashes never played another first-class match after 1883.

Instead of playing cricket, Bligh began a job at the Stock Exchange in London in partnership with a Mr Mayow. His father seems to have fixed it up. Ivo had said that he would do anything to marry Florence, even work as a clerk, and was ready to put his shoulder to the wheel. Yet he could not bring himself to do so. The job was not well paid, and he had to borrow a house for himself and Florence to live in. Depression set in, exacerbated when Florence had a miscarriage in May 1885. They went to Scotland for a month to recuperate at Loch Assynt in the Sutherland mountains. Leisure, in particular fishing, suited him more than work did. Ivo wrote happily to his father: 'Florrie has made a great success with the trout and has been much praised by Duncan who says Mistress Bligh fishes as well as a gentleman!' Family tradition has it that Florence hooked a 35 lb salmon with her first cast on the River Boyne which flows through the old Darnley estate in County Meath, and it was for a long time the record for that stretch of water.

By August of the following year, 1885, Ivo was ready to escape from England, and a daily job in the City, and emigrate to Australia.

My dear Father,
I have not been at all well lately with this city life and have quite made up my mind that the best and in fact only course for me is to throw it up as soon as possible. From the first, though I said nothing about it, the work of a stockjobber was most distasteful to me and now it has come to the point that I have been compelled to come out of the house several times in the course of the day to keep from fainting. The fact is it is madness for a delicate man to attempt it, the standing, bad air, excitement are too much altogether and I honestly believe would about kill me in a couple of years were I to stick to it. The business is a detestable one from beginning to end and besides that I can already see by no means sure to be sufficiently paying to be worth any sacrifice. I am positive that no City life will ever agree with me. From enquiries I have lately made and also what I saw during my travels I fully believe that the most profitable investment for my money and most healthy employment for myself lies in the Country that has already brought me my greatest blessing, in Australia.

Bligh's idea was that he should invest in a sheep station in Australia. Common sense prevailed, and the general hope was that something more suitable for a self-confessed 'delicate man' would be found in the city of Melbourne, where the Clarkes were so influential. The couple set off before the end of 1885 and found a pretty single-storey house at Powlett Street close to the Melbourne Cricket Ground. He took on some part-time work at an art gallery, but this too did not agree with him, although he had tried painting landscapes. Financial worries remained, and soon the size of his family was going to increase as Florence was pregnant again. On 11 March 1886, he wrote home: 'At present we are looking for servants without success – out here they are terribly expensive and scarce – a cook's wages never less than £40 and a housemaid's £35 per annum! Rather an increase on English customs.'

The ladies of Australia had offered sympathy to Bligh from the moment he landed, if not on the *Peshawur*. Australian men were not so sympathetic. Andrew Clarke, Sir William's brother, was obviously detailed to have a man-to-man talk with Bligh, to tell him to snap out of it, to tell him to get on his penny-farthing. 'Fight feelings of fatigue by doing more exercise' was the Clarke advice, specifically two hours of exercise per day. Bligh could not bring himself to heed it. He wrote to his father about being homesick in Melbourne – heaven knows what he would have felt like at a sheep station in the outback, without servants to do the hard work – and went on:

> On the whole I know well that I feel my miseries more acutely when among old associations, companions and pursuits, none of which my wretched nervous system will permit me to appreciate and so I am better away from them all. I hope neither you nor mother distress yourselves about me – all doctors agree that I ought to get well and though I have an amount of misery in these late years that no one even F. can realise the look out ahead seems brighter and more hopeful.

The couple's first child, a large and healthy boy called Esme Ivo, raised Bligh's spirits initially. Even though he – not Florence – went for a holiday to the seaside to recuperate after the birth, the depression soon returned. Wealth and health continued to elude him, and in despair he wrote to his father from Rupertswood on 12 January 1887: 'For the last 2 months I have been so much worse again that I really hardly know what to do. I have gone down almost a stone in weight and from being just under 11 stone as I have been most of the time out here am now hardly 10 stone. They [doctors] lay the fault at the door of my digestive organs principally but hold out hopes of better things.' After much discussion with their friends at Rupertswood it was decided the couple should return to England the following month.

Ivo and Florence Bligh lived first at Brighton, in the fashionable setting of Palmeira Avenue, and here their second son Noel was born. Their financial concerns however were only increased. Ivo's mother, Lady Darnley, had by now mellowed at least on paper and confided to her daughter-in-law: 'You know how unhappy I am at you and Ivo being so poor. You are so good at making the best of things.' One task which Bligh did take on in 1888 was to become the Honorary Secretary and Honorary Treasurer of the County Cricket Council, a new and short-lived body which MCC had set up in the hope that the first-class counties would organise themselves. It collapsed soon afterwards when its promoter Lord Harris was sent to India to become the Governor of Bombay. Becoming President of Kent CCC, as Bligh did in 1892, did not pay either.

Bligh gave his longest known interview to the *Cricket Field* in 1894. He was asked whether he had played at all since giving up the game at the end of the 1883 season. He replied:

> I believe I am correct in saying that I have not had a bat in my hands since then, except twice last year, when I played in Scotland, but had to have someone to run for me. It was a most curious experience, for I felt exactly as if I were taking part in a game of which I knew absolutely nothing. However, I must have had some idea of what I ought to do, for I managed, somehow or other, to make 60 in one of the matches.

This sounds like an old man speaking, not one of 35.

Amid the despondent talk about his own health during the interview there is a light.

> After leaving Cambridge I played [cricket] very seldom, and began to despair of ever getting reasonably well until I began to try golf. I began to play it by doctor's orders, and since then I have been ever so much better. I am convinced that if I had known of the game when I first became ill, and had dropped cricket and racquets and tennis, I should have been in perfect health now. In my case it was absolutely necessary to take exercise, and yet not violent exercise. One of my most constant companions at golf is E.F.S. Tylecote, and the game gives me occasional opportunities of meeting my oldest friends – Alfred Lyttelton and A.G. Steel.

Golf alone was not a complete cure. It would seem Bligh needed a purpose in life, and as he could not bring himself to do a daily job, he had to wait until he became the Earl of Darnley. Then he could live at Cobham Hall, with Florence and his two sons (a daughter Dorothy was to follow in 1893), and manage the family estate. He was the second son, however, and when his father died in 1896, the title went to the first son Edward, Lord Clifton. The second half of Ivo's life was turning into as much of a disaster as the first half of it had been a triumph. Depression and frustration were poisoning his system.

Florence began keeping a diary, apparently for companionship as much as anything. On 5 September 1898 she wrote: 'Ivo unkind and a wound made never to be forgotten. One's efforts are never taken notice of and one's love is constantly slighted – it must kill it in time.' Even her Australian robustness and resilience were being taxed. It may have been around this time that her religious faith became strong. Florence was 'more than a little friendly with God', recalled her future daughter-in-law Rosemary in her ninetieth year. Rosemary married Esme, who became Lord Clifton and then the Ninth Earl of Darnley.

The following day, 6 September, Florence confided to her diary, as she could never have done by word of mouth in Victorian society: 'Certainly a miserable day. Ivo unkind at night and his mother a scene in morning. In life nothing is sadder than never getting the credit for trying – only God knows how I have tried in this family to overcome my many faults but the cold nature and criticism knocks all love away and fills one with despair. I understand what drove Mary to sleep now.'

This last sentence is a reference to Ivo's sister. Mary, unmarried, drowned herself in one of the ponds in Cobham Park in 1896 at the age of 30. Victorian inhibition did not allow any more information about the suicide to leak out.

By 1900 the darkest period had passed. What they had been through, with young children, cannot have been so different from the ups and downs of many couples. They rented a small house in Suffolk, at Little Glemham near Saxmundham, and began to go out as a family. Florence, as well as Ivo, played golf. They played croquet together too. They went cycling with their sons around the flat country lanes. Ivo, never a city man, managed some digging in the garden and golf with his daughter in the meadow beside their house. Florence played the guitar and piano.

In the summer of 1900 the Blighs bought a house, Pettistree Lodge, not far from Glemham. But their quiet country life was about to be disturbed. The years of leadership – the training he had as the cricket captain of Cambridge University, Kent and England – were about to be put to proper use. Fulfilment was going to replace frustration.

When Ivo's father, the Sixth Earl of Darnley, had died in 1896, he had been succeeded by Ivo's elder brother, Edward, Lord Clifton. If cricketers play in a way which reflects their personality, Clifton, as he was normally known, was a prime example. He was wild and paranoid as a person and as a fast round-arm bowler. At Eton he was in the XI in 1869 and 1870 and did much to win the match against Harrow in the latter year, no doubt scaring a few opposing pupils with his speed and personality. *Lillywhite's Companion* in 1871 described him as 'a fast slinging bowler, but too unsteady to excel; a hard hitter and useful bat in a style peculiar to himself'. Pretty effective though: in 1870 he was Eton's leading wicket-taker with 37 wickets at 12 runs each, as well as their leading bowler of wides. For Kent Clifton played six first-class matches, while his last first-class game was for MCC in 1880.

Thereafter Clifton had no conventional form of activity into which he could channel his paranoia. He was not only tall, as most of the Blighs were, and bulky; he was also academically gifted, as most of them were too. Both his father and mother would have swept him under the carpet, but Clifton was not to be kept quiet when he got a bee in his bonnet. Indeed the family history, *The Lords of Cobham Hall*, says he frequently had a whole swarm of them in his bonnet, and had a ferocious temper to boot. His mother referred to Clifton's 'outrageous theories', and he was always firing off letters to the press to vent them. Being a Bligh, these theories often concerned health issues. The biggest bee in his bonnet concerned smallpox vaccination. Towards the end of the nineteenth century research was starting to show that after half a century of vaccination, smallpox was spreading rather than being eradicated. Clifton joined the Anti-Immunisation League and became its most vociferous supporter. In the end compulsory vaccination was abandoned in 1906.

Clifton's own health increasingly became a matter of concern. He suffered from delusions and paranoia, frequently fell into a trance-like state, and would have been diagnosed as a schizophrenic by a modern doctor. He considered having electric shock treatment – this a couple of decades before it was tried as a treatment in the First World War. Failing that, possibly the best remedy would have been to bowl long fast spells, and perhaps play rugby in winter.

His younger brother Ivo, with his tact and diplomacy, was better than most at handling Clifton. In 1886 Bligh wrote to his father: 'I never answer his controversial questions or remarks otherwise than in a general way unless I see a very easy and matter of fact way of doing so . . . his suspicions are always so groundless that in my opinion they are harmless and I make but light of them.'

In 1896 Clifton, aged 46, succeeded to the Cobham estates in Kent and Ireland as the Seventh Earl, but continued to alienate his family. He had always been a bachelor but a whirlwind romance led him to marry a much younger woman by the name of Jemima Blackwood. An enormous engagement party was held at Cobham Hall at which Ivo and Florence were conspicuously absent. Ivo's widowed mother forced herself to go, as it was the only opportunity to meet her future daughter-in-law before the wedding. She reported to Florence: 'I thought I must see her (Jemima) before the 26th. I like her very much – she was very nice to me. It was a formidable House party and I was very shy. The butler and Clifton were filling up a narrow door and I nearly fell into the arms of the butler!'

Early in 1900 a daughter was born to the new couple. In her own right this baby inherited the ancient Barony of Clifton of Leighton Bromswold, which dates back to 1608. But strange, even suspicious, things began to happen, as if her father had not been strange enough already. When the new couple spent their summer in Ireland at Clifton Lodge, the Seventh Earl complained of feeling unwell, and not in any imaginary way as a problem with his kidneys was discovered. It was thought wise that he should return to Cobham, where he arrived back on 2 October 1900. Further complications set in, however, including bronchitis.

The rest of the drama was recorded by Florence in her diary:

October 15th Clifton very seriously ill – no better
18th C no better, weaker and more dropsy – bad signs
20th Very bad accounts of C, fear no hope
31st Mrs H and I were going to luncheon when telegram came for me telling me of poor Clifton's sudden death at midnight – told Ivo quietly and we left Benhall driving home and Ivo went to London and Cobham arriving 11.30 very tired but everyone had gone to bed. November 1st I went to Rectory and stayed the night, a peaceful happy time – a dreamland of what reality might become dawned on me – thank god for such dreams!

Ivo Bligh had become the Eighth Earl of Darnley. Florence, the seventh child of a police magistrate in Australia, had become the Countess of Darnley.

10
Fulfilment

Florence's diary for the year 1900 shows her enthusiasm over their unexpected change of fortune to be much greater than Ivo's. He was not an ambitious man and his inherently shy and melancholic nature ill suited him to a life in the public eye, although his leadership skills during the 1882/83 tour of Australia clearly showed he could more than rise to the occasion when required to do so. For the first time in many years Bligh had been happy and relaxed, pottering about at Pettistree Lodge, enjoying a relatively simple country life. He was President of MCC in 1900, which would have been notoriety enough.

Moreover, Bligh already had a good idea that the family estates, especially those in Ireland, were severely compromised financially. He had written to his father from Australia on the matter back in 1886, when the Irish Home Rule debate had been at its most acerbic:

> Of course I do not know your particular affairs sufficiently to judge what effect the change of law would have on them but I cannot help thinking that if I was a landowner in Ireland and had a fair opportunity of getting rid of my possessions at anything like a fair equivalent I should be only too glad to do so. The landowner in these times seems to be destined to be so beset by adverse legislation not to mention the disadvantage of bad seasons, low prices and co. that really the game seems to be hardly worth the candle.

The Irish Land Acts from 1881 onwards had given tenant farmers in County Meath much greater security over their holdings, fixing their rents for up to fifteen years and allowing them to buy their land if they so wished. From the landowner's perspective, the picture was only slightly rosier in England, where the agricultural depression caused predominantly by cheap imports from America, together with an unprecedented run of poor growing seasons, had been going on for a quarter of a century. This ultimately led to the income from the Cobham estates in Ireland falling by almost half. The outlook was made still gloomier for Bligh in 1900 by Sir William Harcourt's new death duties that had been deliberately designed to hit the great estates. They had now struck Cobham twice in rapid succession, having been introduced shortly before the death of the Sixth Earl, Ivo's father, in 1896.

However the real shock for Ivo was to come after his brother's funeral at Cobham Church on 3 November 1900. According to her diary, Florence travelled down with Ivo's younger brother Arthur by train to meet Ivo there, and she found the occasion 'sad and pathetic'. It was in such marked contrast to the spring day just over a year earlier when the Seventh Earl of Darnley and his young bride had returned home from their honeymoon and the whole village had come out to cheer them. Everyone felt overwhelming pity for Darnley's young widow Jemima and her infant daughter Elizabeth, barely a year old, and whose wreath made from pink roses and violets said simply: 'To dear Dada, from his loving Betty'.

After Clifton's funeral the family returned to Cobham and Florence wrote: 'Desolate and weary – had a cry! Nothing but gloom and sadness. Mother very sweet and kind.' Later that afternoon all the family were summoned together for the reading of the will, and a Pandora's Box it turned out to be. As expected, Ivo was to inherit the Earldom as the male heir, and also all the family estates in Ireland, together with Cobham Hall and the greater part of the estate in Kent; this had been arranged during the time of his father, the Sixth Earl, and there was nothing that the Seventh Earl could have done about it, short of producing a male heir.

It had also been assumed by Bligh, erroneously, that under his father's settlement he would succeed to all the fabulous contents of Cobham Hall itself, whereas it turned out that only the picture collection was included in the arrangement, the rest being mentioned in rather general terms and not legally binding. As a result the Seventh Earl, who understandably wanted to do the best for his young widow and child, left one of the country's finest private collections of furniture, china and tapestries (most of which had been assembled by the Fourth Earl) to Jemima, together with a fair chunk of the Cobham estate and all the surplus family cash. It was an absolute disaster for Bligh and left him financially crippled. As his mother confided to Florence: 'I have been haunted by fears as I know perfectly well Cobham would cost enormous sums to furnish even in the most economical way and I also thought difficult to let." Bligh himself remarked to a reporter from the local paper after his brother's death: 'I am a poor man'.

Florence recorded in her diary that Jemima spent that night at Cobham and dined with the family. One can only imagine the sub-zero atmosphere in a family dining-room which at that time was not renowned for its warm conviviality, particularly as Jemima had already arranged for the removal vans to arrive the following day to start the packing. There is a photograph of Jemima on the occasion of her presentation at Court the year before, and despite being not much older than twenty there is a look of great determination on her face, more than enough to hold her own against the assembled ranks of the Bligh family. Florence wrote: 'It's a great grief to us all to follow the fall of the old home! The old furniture, plate etc all going out of it.'

Florence returned home to her daughter Dorothy, known as Dolly, at Pettistree Lodge 'to explain things to her'. Ivo joined them later that month, the two boys, Esme and Noel, being away at boarding school. The rest of the year was one of mixed emotions for Florence as she confided to her diary:

24th November – sad news about Cobham – must let it.
30th November. Ivo home 5.40 very tired and worried – Jemima coming out in vivid colours! Ivo too sad for words – best be silent.
1st December – Very sad all day about Cobham and family troubles. I had to come out of church and broke down and cried hard to relieve all my feelings. Ivo toothache.

19th December – Went to dear Cobham – a lovely sunny day – most conflicting feelings – the house seemed empty and yet its own beauty made it seem full – at Cobham for 3 weeks. Christmas spent at Pettistree.

31st December – Leave for Cobham 12.45 train – the weather cleared.

I leave Pettistree and the old year – the dear old year that has given so much. I am very grateful and pray to be of it all.

Bligh's mother hated the situation and felt torn between support for Ivo and the desire to see her granddaughter Betty, the infant Baroness of Clifton. She wrote to Florence:

My dearest child

No! I did not enjoy Jemima's party at all and went away as soon as I could. It was disgusting to see all the Cobham things – rows of Custs and Coles's in the red chairs and sofas and other things. I am sure J. did not know you were in London, tho' she might be too ashamed for you to see her robberies . . . I think the most incongruous thing in Jemima's home is the fine Fire Dogs which certainly were more suitable at Cobham and might have been returned there having been unlawfully taken . . . I think there were hardly any miniatures for J. to take except the 4 on a velvet frame which I suppose you saw, and which I had arranged formerly sometime after the year 1860. I think I told you I said to Jemima I longed to pounce on them!

She went on to lament the loss of a family scrap book that she had filled with family keepsakes over the years: 'I think the enemy must have carried it off.'

Solicitors, inevitably, were employed to try and sort out exactly who was entitled to what and yet more money haemorrhaged from the family coffers, but by and large the feisty Jemima got what she wanted. She herself remarried a couple of years later, in 1902, to Admiral Sir Arthur Cavenagh Leveson. Poor little Betty Clifton's future was not destined to be happy. She was to write a few books under the pseudonym 'Lenox Fane', but she was beset by mental problems of one kind or another for most of her short life and never married.

Bligh was in a desperate situation and the only way to stay solvent was to start selling off what was left of the 'family silver'; this was to continue for the rest of his life in spite of heroic efforts to do otherwise. He began by disposing of one of the best Titian 'Old Masters' at Cobham to pay his brother's death duties, and this ended up at the National Gallery with the help of a public subscription. The landed classes of the day had lost confidence in agriculture as a means of providing an income, and all over the country large estates were being split up and sold. His property in Ireland was the first to fall under the hammer and most of the estate in County Meath had gone by the beginning of the First World War, Clifton Lodge itself being sold in 1909. Unfortunately the price realised at about ten shillings per acre did little to improve Bligh's finances, and the Cobham estate records show a steady stream of land sales throughout the first quarter of the twentieth century, culminating in a great sale of 1925 when eighteen of the farms were sold, mostly to tenants. Fortunately the expansion of Rochester gave some comfort to Bligh in that previously marginal agricultural land could be sold for building sites, so over time his money worries began to ease a little.

The new Eighth Earl and his wife soon decided to leave Suffolk and move with their children to Cobham Hall, perhaps because it would have cost too much to refurnish for letting. In any case Florence's Australian warmth helped to take the lingering nineteenth-century chill away from the great old house, and everybody agreed they created an exceptionally happy and relaxed home in which to bring up their three children. Even after his succession to the Darnley title, the name Ivo Bligh seemed to cling to the new Earl in most people's imaginations, but 'Muz' and 'Puz' were the names which the children affectionately coined for their laid-back mother and father. A warm glow seems to radiate from the old sepia photographs of that 'Golden Afternoon' of country house life at Cobham leading up to the First World War. Even 'Lions' the gardener, an image of Old Father Time himself with his long white beard, looks as though he should be holding a large gin and tonic in his right hand rather than secateurs.

The new informal atmosphere created an idyllic place for Esme,

Noel and Dolly to grow up in, in contrast to the days of their grandfather, the Sixth Earl, when they had been left at Cobham for several months while Florence had visited Australia. Then they had been kept locked up in the gloomy children's nurseries with their viewless windows for far too long. Now Noel and his sister could run races down Rocking Horse Gallery – so named for the grey and white pair that lived there – or sneak into the organ loft in the Gilt Hall to see the ghost that Dolly was sure could be found lurking in the shadows. Bligh was more like a kindly older brother to his children than a stern patriarch, and delighted in having the odd practical joke played on him. He was a great ornithologist after the Victorian tradition, and there was a magnificent collection of stuffed birds and blown eggs in the hallway leading from the cannonaded entrance arch at Cobham. One day Dolly was given some coloured chocolate birds' eggs and, having put them in a nest in the garden, she excitedly called 'Puz' over to see the rare specimens, at which point she greedily popped them in her mouth.

After 1900 Florence began eclipsing her husband more and more in terms of personal achievement, although he would have been the last person in the world to complain. She came into her own as a hostess and her confident Australian style complemented Ivo's quieter, more retiring character. It is said he had a very gentle voice, and people who visited Cobham came away with memories of them both to treasure for the rest of their lives. 'There was none of the austerity in his character so often found amongst members of the aristocracy' said the family history *The Lords of Cobham Hall.*

In this way, the relationship between Ivo and Florence mirrored that between England and Australia at cricket. It was not, *au fond,* a rivalry. It was a symbiotic relationship, a partnership, even a union, with elements of rivalry. If England, and Ivo, held the upper hand at first, on grounds of seniority, Australia and its countrywoman Florence became the more dominant partners – if not greatly so – in the course of time. Above all, neither could live without the other: neither Ivo nor Florence, and neither England nor Australia so far as cricket was concerned.

Music continued to play an important role in Florence's life and the Gilt Hall was frequently used for charity events at which she or Dolly would play the piano, together with a professional musician or two. She had a go at composing some hymns, also a song called 'Content', and a couple of her Waltzes were published, including 'Southern Cross' and 'Bonheur', the second of which she wrote for the 'coming out' festivities of Dolly. She became very friendly with Clara Butt, who at over 6ft tall was the most famous of all Edwardian contraltos, and 'that magnificent creature', as Florence called her, sang Elgar's 'Sea Pictures' on one of these occasions. Through Florence, Clara Butt met and married the singer Kennerley Rumford; and Dolly, aged seven, was bridesmaid alongside an equally young page boy by the name of Ivor Novello. In 1907 Clara Butt was encouraged by Florence to make a musical tour of Australia and while discussing her programmes with the Australian diva Dame Nellie Melba she was famously told by her to 'sing 'em muck – it's all they understand'!

The new Countess loved writing, carrying on an enormous correspondence with people from all over the world, and several of her short stories appeared in magazines of the day. As early as 1898 she mentions writing a book in her diary, but nothing was published until 1907 when in collaboration with a friend she wrote 'Elma Trevor'. It was no best-seller, but she did manage to buy a satinwood cabinet with the proceeds. She also became friendly with Rudyard Kipling through her work with the Royal Literary Fund. She put the same enthusiasm into her painting, and her watercolours of the bluebells and rhododendrons in Cobham woods helped to raise funds for local charities. She became quite good for an amateur who had taken art up relatively late in life, and was never without her paintbox on holiday at Aviemore in Scotland or in France.

The high-minded tone at the Hall was meanwhile being undermined by Arthur (Ivo's younger brother, who came to live at Cobham). A bachelor, Uncle Arty had lived in Paris during the 1890s and *la belle epoque*, and had amassed a large collection of erotic books and magazines, according to Ivo and Florence's daughter-in-law Rosemary. After Arthur's death, the fate of his collection remained a mystery. Finally, Ivo's eldest son Esme found the erotica stashed away in the family chapel, the last place Florence would have expected it to be.

Florence took her charity work very seriously, as did many others of her class and generation. She was sometimes criticised privately for somewhat overdoing the 'Mother Bountiful' role; she liked people to know just how benevolent she was and to praise her accordingly, but she undoubtedly helped a great many needy people in the process. In 1905 she hosted her first Arts and Crafts fair at Cobham Hall and three years later she established a centre for lace-making in the village, which eventually was extended to include eleven further villages.

Through her charity work Florence became very friendly with Queen Mary, the consort of King George V. They could empathise with each other in that both were brought up in families who had fallen on hard times, only to marry into a much higher social strata. Queen Mary would regularly visit Cobham but the family had to be very careful to hide any small, choice items of furniture from her eagle eye. Royal protocol demanded that anything admired by H.R.H. had to be presented to her, and she was well known up and down the country for exploiting this prerogative. On one occasion Queen Mary arrived with her young daughter-in-law Princess Elizabeth – later to be known as 'the Queen Mother' – and Dolly was also present. The four of them went for a walk in the Cobham bluebell woods, which were just then at their best. Florence and Queen Mary strode on ahead, talking nineteen to the dozen, completely oblivious to anybody or anything. Elizabeth turned to Dolly and said: 'Look at those two old dears trampling over all these beautiful bluebells without a care in the world!'

Florence's best works were done soon after the start of the First World War. She and her husband decided to do their bit for the war effort by opening up Cobham Hall as a military hospital and over the next four years over 2,000 Australians passed through it. Florence acted as Matron and wrote in her diary at the beginning of 1915:

The first 6 months of war over – Noel safe thank God. Our hospital a great resource and solace helping the poor wounded men and giving to them love and care for what they have given the KING AND COUNTRY. Nurse Schofield kind and nice – not altogether popular but a good head and manager. Dolly done good works and loved by her boys. The interest has absorbed Ivo and he has taken great interest. The War is drawing out the best in all and the courage and patience of all is wonderful. Xmas tired me out – it was a strenuous time. Xmas a true family party, shooting and work at the hospital. I had to rest 2 or 3 days. Friends true and loving helped through the year. A bad epidemic of Flue brought here by Constance. 14 cases are fatal in early New Year – a great trial. Ivo, Doll and I got it mildly. Ivo's lasted long and tediously. Noel wounded in head 25th September – home and saw him following Friday. Doll's engagement (to Dan Peploe) a happy one – he is young and perhaps not strong enough nature but a real dear – his parents came New Year's day and like both. All happy.

The Australian Prime Minister, Mr W.M. Hughes, visited Cobham over Christmas 1917, and during dinner a couple of young and ambitious airmen asked Florence to try and persuade Mr Hughes to let them have the privilege of making the first attempt to fly from England to Australia. Florence charmed the Prime Minister into agreeing to do what he could; and soon after the end of the war a Vickers Vimy long range bomber with Captain Ross Smith MC, DFC, AFC at its controls, accompanied by Lieutenant Keith Smith and two air mechanics, 'clattered into the skies over southern England and into aviation history'. They arrived eventually at Darwin, and a memorial inscription at Adelaide Airport records how they landed on 10 December 1919, having flown 11,060 miles through France, Italy, Crete, Egypt, Palestine, Mesopotamia, Persia, India, Burma, Siam, Malaya, and the Dutch East Indies. These four pioneers of civil aviation won a price of £10,000 from the Commonwealth Government for being the first to fly from England to Australia in less than 30 days, and the two officers were knighted by King George V in recognition of their tremendous feat. The British Prime Minister summed up their achievement by saying: 'your flight shows how the inventions of war can advance the progress of peace.'

Both Florence and Ivo worked unceasingly for the hospital but his health was never quite the same after the War – he suddenly looked much older and some suspected it shortened his life. Florence's efforts were more publicly recognised when she was created a Dame of the British Empire in 1919. She continued her interest in hospitals after her own at Cobham had closed its doors, and she became President of both the Linen League at St Bartholomew's Hospital, Rochester, and the Cobham and Luddesdowne Nursing Association for many years.

In spite of his initial misgivings, Ivo settled down to life at Cobham with all its responsibilities very happily. He later grew a distinguished beard and jokingly remarked: 'I expect Cobham will in future be known as "Beaver's Bothy"!' He enjoyed a harmonious relationship with all the tenants on the Cobham estate, so much so that he himself took on the cultivation of the Lodge Farm until shortly before his death, and he was fond of saying how he felt 'at one with his brother farmers'. Ivo continued to be very fond of the gun and he ran a further six farms as a reasonably lucrative shooting syndicate business of which he was a member. In 1925 he set up the Cobham Hall Estate Company Ltd to help save what remained of the estate for his son Esme, and generally every effort was made to shore up the family finances. This was the period when Americans were voraciously buying up all the Old Masters that came on to the English market and as a result prices were at an absolute premium, particularly for good English portraits from aristocratic houses. Ivo felt it prudent to take advantage of this strong market and consequently Christie's held a massive sale of many of the choicest remaining paintings from the Cobham collection on 1 May 1925. There were 92 lots in the sale and it produced for the time a quite remarkable total of £70,758, 9s, 0d. There were no fewer than five Titians, including 'Danae', five Van Dykes, five Lelys, four Reynolds, four Gainsboroughs, three Canalettos, two Hoppners, one Raphael and a Rubens. Imagine the furore today if such a collection ended up sailing off to New York, where the masterpieces can still be found in collections such as the Frick.

In 1923 Ivo and Florence decided to build a smaller house for themselves overlooking Cobham Park in nearby Shorne Woods. Cobham Hall was becoming prohibitively expensive to run. It required a full-time building company to maintain the fabric, and in its heyday more than 60 people were employed just around the house itself. Cobham was let to an enormous, very wealthy and elderly American lady, who delighted in welcoming with open arms all of Ivo and Florence's grandchildren into her gargantuan feather bed and giving them expensive trifles such as diamond-studded sets of dice. Puckle Hill was rather a gloomy house in the Elizabethan style, made from red brick and vast quantities of oak cut from the estate. Ivo referred to it as his 'cottage', although by today's standards it was pretty large, and Florence, who was an avid gardener, used her ability as a water diviner to design the terraced gardens. Ivo was a deeply religious man in his own quiet way, and over the doorway to his new house he had placed the Latin motto 'Deo Opti Maxi' or 'To God, the best and greatest'.

He also took seriously his public role beyond the confines of the Cobham estate and served on the Kent County Council for nearly twenty years, chairing the Parliamentary and Public Health Committee. He was a J.P. and involved in a myriad of charities associated with the North Kent area. The Darnley title itself was Irish and did not confer an automatic seat in the House of Lords, but in 1905 he was elected a representative peer for Ireland and occasionally spoke in the Upper Chamber. His old friend and captain Lord Harris wrote:

> Some of his best work was during the war as county director of the Kent V.A.D.'s [the volunteer nursing division]. I persuaded him to suppress his diffidence, and to take charge of that most important institution, and the charm of his method of command, the velvet glove, resulted in the foundation of a system which carried through to the end of the war, and won the highest recommendation from the Director of the Red Cross Society.

Golf continued to be Ivo's main sporting activity. In 1909 he became the first President of the Mid-Kent Golf Club and arranged for his old friend Alfred Lyttelton to open it with Mr Balfour, who had recently stepped down as Prime Minister. He became Captain of St George's at Sandwich, and in 1920 granted a ten-year lease on part of the Deer Park at Cobham for an annual peppercorn rent of £1 to the Rochester and Cobham Park Golf Club.

To the end of his life, however, Ivo considered the urn containing the Ashes to be his most prized possession and his captaincy of England to be his finest achievement. The urn was always kept on the mantelpiece in his study, but unfortunately no photograph has survived of it 'in situ'. It seems to have been all too vulnerable when Ivo's back was turned. In old age his butler recalled an occasion when the housemaid came to him at Cobham saying: 'You know that old vase thing that stands on the mantelpiece in His Lordship's room – well I knocked it over and found it was full of old ash stuff, so I gave it a good clean and polish before putting it back.' According to the butler, after calling the girl a few choice names, he went and scraped some wood ash from the fireplace and put it in the urn, and neither Lord Darnley nor his family were told of the incident.

A somewhat similar story was recalled by the late Elinor Bullen Smith, sister of Esme's second wife Nancy – Esme now being Lord Clifton or 'Clif'. Elinor remembers being shown the urn by her sister on a visit to Cobham when the rest of the family were out of the room, and Nancy accidentally knocked it off the mantelpiece into the grate. Not only was the urn slightly chipped in the process but the cork popped out, spilling the contents all over the hearth. Nancy was horrified, but quickly topped the urn up with ash from the dying fire, saying: 'For heaven's sake don't tell Clif!'

History does not relate where Ivo kept the little velvet bag, embroidered with the date 1883 and given to him in Australia by Mrs Ann Fletcher, that accompanies the urn. More than likely it was carefully wrapped in tissue paper and put in some locked drawer, for it seems in remarkably good condition with very little fading.

Ivo died in his sleep, aged 68, at Puckle Hill in April 1927 and was found by his valet at 8.30 one Sunday morning. He had been playing golf in Cobham Park only the day before. The tributes poured in, and one old villager who was interviewed at 'The Leather Bottle', Cobham's local pub, summed up the feeling in the village by saying: 'He was more like a brother to all of us than anything else. He was a man who couldn't say no to you whatever you asked for – he always put his hand in his pocket for anything that came along.'

On his death, the urn containing the Ashes (of one sort or another) was given by Florence to MCC to keep in a glass case in the Long Room at Lord's, before the Museum was founded. There was no mention of the urn in Bligh's will, as *Wisden* asserts. Adam, the present Earl of Darnley, has checked the will and found no reference. At Lord's it has stayed, except for the occasional outing, as for the dinner in honour of Woodfull's touring team in 1930, or Australia's bicentenary, or the MCC exhibition in Australia.

Florence carried on at Puckle much as usual after Ivo's death, surrounded by friends and family. She had only ever made one further visit back home to Australia, in 1904, when she had sailed aboard the P and O liner *Ophir* with the eleven-year-old Dolly, but her sisters and their children were frequent visitors to England and she was genuinely very fond of them – provided they remembered at all times that she was the 'Countess of Darnley'. She loved listening to music right up to the end of her life, and on one occasion at Puckle her sister complained about the noise which her grandson Tony was making on his saxophone, only to be told in no uncertain terms to 'like it or lump it'. Florence's daughter-in-law remembers her being increasingly belligerent as she grew older, but generally her grandchildren loved her and she loved them. Her relationship with her daughter Dolly was more problematic and they rarely, if ever, saw each other during the last ten years of her life. Florence left Puckle Hill at the beginning of the war and went to live with her old friend Lady Rathcreden at Bellehatch Park, Henley-on-Thames, and it was here that she died on Wednesday 30 August 1944.

The final resting place of Ivo and Florence is in a quiet corner of Cobham churchyard, which in early summer is surrounded by a profusion of cow-parsley and poppies, an untouched patch in the larger Kentish landscape. There is no grand edifice or memorial to the Darnleys in the village they knew and loved, and the family graves are for the most part hidden in a shady corner of the churchyard where few visitors think to venture. A certain diffidence seems to linger even after Ivo's death.

Yet Ivo Bligh will forever be the England cricket captain who first returned with the urn, the urn; and the welkin will ring loud, the great crowd feel proud, when a successor comes back with the urn.

Appendix A
Whatever happened to . . . Bligh's Tourists

Richard Barlow came far closer to longevity than the other three professionals in Bligh's party, mainly because he kept himself fit. On three tours of Australia he did not miss a match. He represented Lancashire at cricket until 1891, when he was forty, and at football as a goalkeeper. Not only on the boat home did he win a sprint race. From 1894 until the First World War he was a first-class umpire. He wrote a book of memoirs and collected cricket memorabilia, and died aged 68.

William Barnes died in 1899, aged 46. Worsening alcoholism contributed to the ending of his Nottinghamshire contract in 1894. He then became landlord of the 'Angel Inn' in Mansfield Woodhouse. At least he outlived his elder brother Thomas, who had also played for Nottinghamshire, and died of typhoid aged 24. William Barnes will always remain though one of the best all-rounders England ever had, as he averaged 23 with the bat and 15 with the ball in his 21 Tests against Australia.

William Bates was hit in the eye by a stray ball while practising at Melbourne on the 1887/88 tour to Australia under George Vernon. He never played again. His career was over at the age of 32. He tried to commit suicide, but did not succeed, and recovered enough to do a little coaching and play some club cricket. In December 1900 he insisted on attending the funeral of another cricketer from Lascelles Hall, John Thewlis, caught a cold and died the following month, aged 45, to be buried beside Thewlis. In his fifteen Tests, all against Australia, he averaged 27 with the bat and 16 with the ball.

Charles Leslie died in 1921, aged 59, a wealthy man whose interests included a shipping business. He was the great-grandfather of Matthew Fleming, the Kent all-rounder and banker. Although he played for Oxford University in 1883 after returning from Australia, he played little cricket thereafter and bowled even less. His 144 against New South Wales remained the highest of his four first-class centuries. His four Test wickets, including his spell of three wickets in the First Test at Melbourne, constituted half of his first-class haul.

The English touring team of 1884/85 in Australia were devastated to hear that **Fred Morley** had died on 28 September 1884, aged 33. The cause was given as congestion and dropsy but there was little doubt that the broken rib he had suffered aboard the *Peshawur* was the start of his decline. Having finally been diagnosed properly in Australia, he was given medical treatment at MCC's expense back in England, but could only play a couple more matches, one each for Nottinghamshire and MCC, before his death. In 1885 North played South at Lord's for the benefit of Morley's widow and children.

Walter Read remained a cricketer all his life. He became assistant secretary of Surrey so that he could play for them as an amateur. In all he scored over 22,000 first-class runs at the fine average for the time of 32. He wrote a book about the game, a staid chronicle of his career, and even took a benefit to help pay his bills. He twice captained England, once in Australia in the fiasco two-tour winter of 1887/88, and once in South Africa, and won both his Tests. He was still with Surrey, as coach, when he died in 1907 aged 51.

Charles Studd, although he did not seek fame, became one of the most renowed of all Christian missionaries by the time he died in the Congo in 1931, uttering as his final word 'Hallelujah'. After captaining Cambridge in the 1883 season he virtually gave up the game, turned to religion, and became one of 'the Cambridge Seven' who went to China in 1885. He dressed and lived as a Chinese, gave away his large inheritance, and married a missionary from Ulster, Priscilla Stewart. In 1910 he decided to evangelise the region between the Nile and Lake Chad. He was made 'Chevalier of the Royal Order of the Lion' by the King of the Belgians for his services to Congo.

George Studd was called to the Bar after leaving Cambridge, whom he captained in 1882, but never studied as a barrister. He became seriously ill and decided after his illness on a less worldly existence. On his way back from a visit to Australia he went to visit his brother Charles, who was a member of the China Inland Mission, and was persuaded to become a missionary himself. From 1891 until his death in 1945 he worked in Los Angeles, where he defied convention by worshipping in a mixed black and white congregation.

Allan Steel lived until the age of 55. Until his death, in 1914, he was Recorder of Oldham, after giving up his practice as a barrister in Liverpool. In 1902 he was President of MCC. It would have been very difficult for him to live up to the glories of his youth, when he was hailed as the only schoolboy good enough to bowl for England. In his four years at Cambridge he averaged 32 with the bat and 10 with the ball. He wrote several insightful chapters in the *Cricket* volume of the Badminton library.

Edward Tylecote was a safe pair of hands in every sense save that of love. At the same time that his captain was wooing, he became engaged to Miss Clarke at Rupertswood – and dropped her. He returned to England and played little cricket after 1883, when he became only the sixth batsman to hit a century for the Gentlemen against the Players at Lord's. He played a lot of golf, however, and often with Bligh, with whom he stayed at Cobham Hall. After being a Fellow of St John's, Oxford, he became a maths tutor at the Royal Military Academy. In 1905 he married Annie Louisa Robson, the daughter of a barrister. He was the longest-living Oxford cricket captain at his death in 1938 at the age of 88. Although he left no children, he bequeathed a large collection of butterflies and moths to the Ashmolean museum in Oxford.

George Vernon, although he was not a professional, also died at a relatively young age, aged 46, when he contracted malarial fever in the Gold Coast. His Test on Bligh's tour remained his only Test match but he did captain an English cricket team in Australia – and married an Australian woman, a Miss Jeffray, of Toorak, Melbourne. In 1887/88 two sides, one professional, the other amateur, toured Australia simultaneously, which was absurd and financially disastrous. Lord Hawke led the amateur side, but when he had to go home on the death of his father, Vernon took over the captaincy – and stepped aside when the two teams combined to play a Test. Vernon also led a team to India in 1889/90, but he never became very good at cricket as his bat was not straight in defence. His first-class career batting average was 19. He was better at rugby for Blackheath and England.

Australia's Players

Alexander Bannerman was determined to be the opposite of his elder brother, almost from the moment that Charles was born in England and Alex – or 'Alick' – in Sydney. Whereas Charles was dashing and dissolute, Alex was dour and dapper. In the 1891/92 Test at Sydney he batted seven and a half hours for 91, scoring 5 runs off the 204 balls bowled at him by William Attewell. He was hailed as the finest of Australian stonewallers, and made five tours of England.

Jack Blackham set a new standard for wicketkeepers by dispensing with a long-stop and standing up to almost every bowler with his beard over the bails. He became entirely dependable, whether as a keeper or a bank clerk or a left-handed batsman. In his first-class career he made the outstanding number of 454 dismissals, more than a third of them stumpings. He captained Australia in eight Tests, including on the 1893 tour of England which was his last.

George Bonnor never did reconcile himself to being an all-out hitter. He played in 17 Tests and his batting average was the same figure. He made one Test century though, in 1884/85 at Sydney, when he came in at 119 for six and scored 128 out of 169 runs added, enough to turn the match. He fully lived up to his reputation as the Australian Hercules in up-country cricket, as when he scored 267 not out in two hours for Bathurst against Oriental C.C. He was a brilliant fielder too, like Andrew Flintoff, for one of his size.

Harry Boyle passed his prime after the 1882/83 series. He went on two more tours of England, in 1884 and 1888, but at the age of 41 took only ten wickets on his last tour. He will always be remembered though for his fielding at silly mid-on, especially to Spofforth, as well as for his round-arm medium-pace. Like his team-mates, he lived to a greater age than his professional counterparts in England's teams.

By the time he made his first tour of England in 1886, **Edwin Evans** was well past his peak and no English spectator would have believed that he had once been rated as Spofforth's equal or superior as a bowler. His all-round ability lived on though as a horseman in the outback. The bush poet 'Banjo' Paterson saw Evans shoot a kangaroo when riding at full speed and thought Evans' eye for a ball was the secret.

Tom Garrett, at 18, was the youngest man to play for Australia when he was selected for the first-ever Test in 1876/77, and thus he remains. He never fulfilled though his all-round promise as a batsman and medium-pacer: his Test batting average was 12, his bowling average 26, very high for the time. He became renowned though as a wise old bird when he captained New South Wales, and wiser still as he lived until 1943, the longest-surviving of all the players in the first of all Tests.

Amazing that after all these years no Australian cricketer has matched **George Giffen's** feat of 10,000 first-class runs and 1,000 first-class wickets. But then he was known as the South Australian 'W.G.' and was as much the pillar of his state as Grace was for Gloucestershire. He did not even have seasons in county cricket with which to swell his figures, although he did make five tours of England. After the 1882/83 series Giffen also went on to become the first Australian to do the Test double of 1,000 runs and 100 wickets.

Tom Horan was a notable batsman, who captained Australia twice, but he became more notable still as a journalist – the first Australian cricket-writer who had himself been a Test player. As 'Felix' of the

Australasian he hung round the pavilion and dressing-room in Melbourne and both passed on the lore to players and listened to what was new from them. In so doing he educated the Australian cricket public to a higher standard than the English, a gap which has perhaps only been closed in recent years.

It is not apparent that **Hugh Massie** recovered from being dropped, firstly down the order, then from the Australian team, during the 1882/83 series. As his 55 in the Oval Test of 1882 remained his one notable innings, in nine Tests, it would seem he did not recover and his ability went unfulfilled. He became a banker by profession, instead of being the 'banker' he could have been in the Australian side, taking the new ball apart.

Percy McDonnell was one of the few Australian cricketers as short-lived as an English professional. He was not yet 38 when he died of a heart attack, leaving a wife, two children and a third still to be born. Ironically, he was a doctor. In his 19 Tests he scored 950 runs at the exceptional average for the time of 28, coming to the fore on bad pitches.

William Midwinter, born in England in the Forest of Dean, emigrated to Australia when he was nine. As he was a fine all-rounder, he became involved in a tug-of-war. On Australia's 1878 tour he was playing for the tourists at Lord's when W.G. Grace burst into the dressing-room and took him off to play for Gloucestershire at the Oval. The tug-of-war continued as he played four Tests for England against Australia, and eight Tests for Australia against England. He died aged 39 in a Melbourne asylum, after being driven mad by the deaths of his wife and two young children.

William Murdoch became the prototype of several modern Australian cricketers when he played county cricket as a batsman and captain. After leading Australia on four tours of England, and becoming the first batsman to score a Test double-century, he captained Sussex for seven years as an amateur. He even played for

England, and kept wicket, on a tour of South Africa in 1891/92, when a match there was retrospectively given Test status. C.B. Fry spoke warmly of Murdoch's sense of humour when he captained Sussex, referring to 'how valuable to a touring side were his cheery, sanguine temperament, his promptness and determination, and his happy gift of good fellowship'.

George Palmer's bowling career was effectively ended by a knee injury when he was only 26. He concentrated more on his batting, and played for Tasmania as well as Victoria, but could not match the value of his off-spin in its prime. On the 1886 tour of England he became the first Australian to do the double of 1,000 runs and 100 wickets in a first-class season; and his Test record was 78 wickets in seventeen Tests at 21 apiece. He married Jack Blackham's sister.

In 1885 **Frederick Spofforth** moved from New South Wales to Victoria, where he played for two seasons, then to England, where he played occasionally for Derbyshire and regularly for Hampstead. At the latter club he was photographed, while bowling, for posterity by Beldham, the first great cricket photographer. Spofforth also became the managing director of the Star Tea Company and prospered to the extent that his estate was worth £164,000 when he died in England aged 73. As a businessman who was successful after cricket, as well as a bowler, Spofforth was always exceptional.

And finally:

Martin Cobbett continued to cover cricket and other sports, and he wrote a book in his retirement called *Sporting Notions*, in the foreword of which his wife Alice Cobbett praised him for 'scrupulous fairness'. Some of these notions are rather vague, or concern the quality of beer which was served at cricket matches, but he was specific enough when he said that the greatest ovation he ever heard in sport came at the Oval Test of 1902, first when Gilbert Jessop made his match-winning century, then when George Hirst and Wildred Rhodes saw England through to a one-wicket win over Australia.

Cobbett also looked back fondly on his overseas assignment:

I guess that very seldom has an English company touring in Australia had a better or more enjoyable time than did that which Lord Darnley took out in 1882 at the invitation of the Melbourne Cricket Club . . . While Mr Bligh was in command I do not think that he ever had a wry word with one of the team, nor with any of the opposition except once, and that was when a professor surreptitiously adorned his boots with things like the clamps boys used to use for tree-climbing, intending to make a place for the other end bowler. [Spofforth was still alive when Cobbett wrote his book, so the latter had to be careful.] Lord Darnley was a model cricketer, game to do any mortal thing to make sport and play any part – high, middling, or humble.

Appendix B

1882/83: Australia v. England (1st Test) Melbourne. December 30, January 1, 2. Umpires: J Swift and E H Elliot. Australia won toss. Australia won by nine wickets.

Australia

First innings			Second innings	
A C Bannerman	st Tylecote b Leslie	30	not out	25
H H Massie	c and b C T Studd	4	c and b Barnes	0
W L Murdoch	b Leslie	48	not out	33
T P Horan	c Barlow b Leslie	0		
P S McDonnell	b Bates	43		
G Giffen	st Tylecote b Steel	36		
G J Bonnor	c Barlow b Barnes	85		
J M Blackham	c Tylecote b C T Studd	25		
F R Spofforth	c Steel b Barnes	9		
T W Garrett	c C T Studd b Steel	0		
G E Palmer	not out	0		
	Extras	11	Extras	0
		291	**(one wkt)**	**58**

Fall of wickets 1/5 2/81 3/1 4/96 5/162 6/190 7/251   1/0
8/289 9/289 10/291

Bowling: *First innings*–CT Studd 46–30–35–2; Barnes–30–11–51–2; Steel–33–16–68–2; Barlow–20–6–37–0; Bates–21–7–31–1; Read–8–2–27–0; Leslie–11–1–31–3. *Second innings*–CT Studd–14–11–7–0; Barnes–13–8–6–1; Steel 9–4–17–0; Barlow–4–2–6–0; Bates 13.1–7–22–0.

England

First Innings			Second Innings	
R G Barlow	st Blackham b Palmer	10	b Spofforth	28
Hon Ivo Bligh	b Palmer	0	(5) b Spofforth	3
C F H Leslie	c Garrett b Palmer	4	(7) b Giffen	4
C T Studd	b Spofforth	0	(3) b Palmer	21
A G Steel	b Palmer	27	(4) lbw b Giffen	29
W W Read	b Palmer	19	b Giffen	29
W Bates	c Bannerman b Garret	28	(8) c Massie b Palmer	11
E F S Tylecote	b Palmer	33	(2) b Spofforth	38
G B Studd	run out	7	c Palmer b Giffen	0
W Barnes	b Palmer	26	not out	2
G F Vernon	not out	11	lbw b Plamer	3
	Extras	12	Extras	1
		177		169

Fall of wickets   1/2 2/7 3.8 4/36 5/45 6.96   1/64 2/75 3/105 4/108 5/132 6/150
                  7/96 8/116 9/156 10/177   7/164 8/164 9/164 10/169

Bowling: *First innings*–Spofforth–28–11–56–1; Palmer–52.2–25–65–7; Garrett–27–6–44–1. *Second innings*–Spofforth–41–15–65–3; Palmer–36.1–11–61–3; Garrett–2–1–4–0; Giffen–20–7–38–4.

1882/83: Australia v. England (2nd Test) Melbourne. January 19, 20, 22.
Umpires: J Swift and E H Elliot. England won toss.
England won by an innings and 27 runs.

England

First Innings

R G Barlow	b Palmer	14
C T Studd	b Palmer	14
C F H Leslie	run out	54
A G Steel	c McDonnell b Giffen	39
W W Read	c and b Palmer	75
W Barnes	b Giffen	32
E F S Tylecote	b Giffen	0
Hon Ivo Bligh	b Palmer	0
W Bates	c Horan b Palmer	28
G B Studd	b Palmer	1
F Morley	not out	0
	Extras	10
		294

Fall of wickets   1/28 2/35 3/106 4/131 5/193
6/199 7/199 8/287 9/293 10/294

Bowling: *First innings*–Spofforth–34–11–57–0; Palmer–66.3–25–103–5; Giffen–49–13–89–4; Garrett–34–16–35–0.

Australia

First innings			Second innings		
H H Massie	b Barlow	43	(7) c C T Studd b Barlow	10	
A C Bannerman	b Bates	14	c Bligh b Bates	14	
W L Murdoch	not out	19	(1) b Bates	17	
T P Horan	c and b Barnes	3	(5) c Morley b Bates	15	
P S McDonnell	b Bates	3	(6) b Bates	13	
G Giffen	c and b Bates	0	(8) c Bligh b Bates	19	
G J Bonnor	c Read b Bates	0	(4) c Morley b Barlow	34	
J M Blackham	b Barnes	5	(3) b Barlow	6	
T W Garrett	b Bates	10	c Barnes b Bates	6	
G E Palmer	b Bates	7	c G B Studd b Bates	4	
F R Spofforth	b Bates	0	not out	14	
	Extras	10	Extras	1	
		114		153	

Fall of wickets   1/56 2/72 3/75 4/78 5/78   1/21 2/28 3/66 4/72 5/93 6/104
6/78 7/85 8/104 9/114   7/113 8/132 9/139 10/153
10/114

Bowling: *First innings*– CT Studd 4–1–22–0; Morley–23–16–13–0; Barnes–23–7–32–2; Barlow–22–18–9–1; Bates–26.2–14–28–7. *Second innings*–Morley–2–0–7–0; Barnes–3–1–4–0; Barlow–31–6–67–3; Bates–33–14–74–7.

1882/83: Australia v. England (3rd Test) Sydney. January 26, 27 29, 30
Umpires: J Swift and E H Elliot. England won toss.
England won by 69 runs.

England

First Innings			Second innings	
R G Barlow	c Murdoch b Spofforth	28	(3) c Palmer b Horan	24
C T Studd	c Blackham b Garrett	21	b Spofforth	25
C F H Leslie	b Spofforth	0	(1) b Spofforth	8
A G Steel	b Garrett	17	lbw b Spofforth	6
W W Read	c Massie b Bannerman	66	b Horan	21
W Barnes	b Spofforth	2	lbw b Spofforth	3
E F S Tylecote	run out	66	c Bonnor b Spofforth	0
W Bates	c McDonnell b Spofforth	17	c Murdoch b Horan	4
G B Studd	b Palmer	3	(1) c Garrett b Spofforth	8
Hon Ivo Bligh	b Palmer	13	(9) not out	17
F Morley	not out	2	b Spofforth	0
	Extras	12	Extras	7
		247		123

Fall of wickets   1/41 2/44 3/67 4/69 5/75 6/191   1/13 2/45 3/55 4/87 5/92 6/94
7/223 8/224 9/244 10/247   7/97 8/98 9/115 10/123

Bowling: *First innings*–Giffen–12–3–37–0; Palmer–38–21–38–2; Spofforth–51–19–73–4; Garrett–27–8–54–2; Bannerman–11–2–17–1; McDonnell–4–0–16–0.
Second innings: Palmer–9–3–19–0; Spofforth–41.1–23–44–7; Garrett–13–3–31–0; Horan–17–10–22–3.

Australia

First innings			Second innings	
A C Bannerman	c Bates b Morley	94	c Bligh b Barlow	5
G Giffen	st Tylecote b Bates	41	(b Barlow	7
W L Murdoch	lbw b Steel	19	(c G B Studd b Morley	0
P S McDonnell	b Steel	0	(5) c Bligh b Morley	0
T P Horan	c Steel b Morley	19	(4) run out	8
H H Massie	c Bligh b Steel	1	c C T Studd b Barlow	11
G J Bonnor	c G B Studd b Morley	0	b Barlow	8
J M Blackham	b Barlow	27	b Barlow	26
T W Garrett	c Barlow b Morley	0	(11) b Barlow	0
G E Palmer	c G B Studd b Barnes	7	not out	2
F R Spofforth	not out	0	(9) c Steel b Barlow	7
	Extras	10	Extras	9
		218		83

Fall of wickets   1/76 2/140 3/140 4/176   1/11 2/12 3/18 4/18 5/30 6/33
5/177 6/178 7/196 8/196   7/56 8/72 9/80 10/83
9/218 10/218

Bowling: *First innings*–Morley–34–16–47–4; Barlow–47.1–31–52–1; Bates–45–20–55–1; Barnes–13–6–22–1; CT Studd–14–11–5–0; Steel–26–14–27–3.
Second innings: Morley–35–19–34–2; Barlow–34.2–20–40–7.

1882/83: Australia v. England (4th Test) Sydney. February 17, 19, 20, 21
Umpires: J Swift and E H Elliot. England won toss.
Australia won by four wickets.

England

First Innings			Second innings	
R G Barlow	c Murdoch b Midwinter	2	c Bonnor b Midwinter	20
C T Studd	run out	48	c Murdoch b Midwinter	31
C F H Leslie	c Bonnor b Boyle	17	b Horan	19
A G Steel	not out	135	b Spofforth	21
W W Read	c Bonnor b Boyle	11	b Spofforth	7
E F S Tylecote	b Boyle	5	b Palmer	0
W Barnes	b Spofforth	2	(9) c and b Boyle	20
W Bates	c Bonnor b Midwinter	9	(7) not out	48
Hon Ivo Bligh	b Palmer	19	(8) c Murdoch b Horan	10
G B Studd	run out	3	c Murdoch b Boyle	9
F Morley	b Palmer	0	c Blackham b Palmer	2
	Extras	12	Extras	10
		263		197

Fall of wickets	1/13 2/37 3/110 4/150	1/54 2/55 3/77 4/99 5/100 6/112
	5/156 6/159 7/199 8/236	7/137 8/178 9/192 10/197
	9/263 10/263	

Bowling: *First innings*–Palmer–24–9–52–2; Midwinter–47–24–50–2; Spofforth–21–8–56–1; Boyle–40–19–52–3; Horan–12–4–26–0; Evans–11–3–15–0.
Second innings: Palmer–43.3–19–59–2; Midwinter–23–13–21–2; Spofforth–28–6–57–2; Boyle–23–6–35–2; Horan–9–2–15–2.

Australia

First innings			Second innings	
A C Bannerman	c Barlow b Morley	10	c Bligh b C T Studd	63
G J Bonnor	c Barlow b Steel	87	(3) c G B Studd b Steel	3
W L Murdoch	b Barlow	0	(2) c Barlow b Bates	17
T P Horan	c G B Studd b Morley	4	c and b Bates	0
G Giffen	st Tylecote b Bates	41	b Barlow	7
W E Midwinter	b Barlow	10	(8) not out	8
J M Blackham	b Bates	57	(6) not out	58
G E Palmer	c Bligh b Steel	0		2
E Evans	not out	22	(7) c Leslie b Steel	0
F R Spofforth	c Bates b Steel	1		
H F Boyle	c G B Studd b Barlow	29		
	Extras	15	Extras	18
		262	(six wkts)	199

Fall of wickets	1/31 2/34 3/39 4/113	1/44 2/51 3/51 4/107 5/162 6/164
	5/128 6/160 7/164 8/220	
	9/221 10/262	

Bowling: *First innings*–Barlow–48–21–88–3; Morley–44–25–45–2; Barnes–10–2–33–0; Bates–15–6–24–1; Steel–19–6–34–3; CT Studd–6–2–12–0.
Second innings– Barlow–37.1–20–44–0; Morley–12–9–4–2; Barnes–16–5–22–0; Bates–39–19–52–2; Steel–43–9–49–3; CT Studd–8–4–8–1.

Appendix C

TEST AVERAGES 1882/83

ENGLAND BATTING

	M	I	NO	HA	R	Av
Steel	4	7	1	135*	274	45.66
Read	4	7	0	75	228	32.57
Bates	4	7	1	55	172	28.66
Studd C	4	7	0	48	160	22.86
Tylecote	4	7	0	66	142	20.29
Barlow	4	7	0	28	126	18.00
Leslie	4	7	0	54	106	15.14
Barnes	4	7	1	32	87	14.50
Vernon	1	2	1	11*	14	14.00
Bligh	4	7	1	19	62	10.33
Studd G	4	7	0	9	31	4.43
Morley	3	5	2	2*	4	1.33

ENGLAND BOWLING

	balls	maidens	runs	wickets	average
Leslie	96	19	44	4	11.00
Bates	775	91	286	19	15.10
Morley	588	85	140	8	17.50
Steel	516	53	195	11	17.72
Barlow	1021	123	338	15	22.53
Barnes	452	36	170	6	28.33
Studd C	368	59	89	3	29.66

England scored 1470 runs for 70 wickets at 21.00

AUSTRALIA BATTING

	M	I	NO	HS	R	Av
Bannerman	4	8	1	94	255	36.43
Blackham	4	7	1	58*	204	34.00
Bonnor	4	7	0	87	217	31.00
Boyle	1	1	0	29	29	29.00
Murdoch	4	8	2	48	153	25.50
Giffen	4	7	0	41	162	23.14
Evans	1	2	1	22*	22	22.00
Midwinter	1	2	1	10	18	18.00
McDonnell	3	5	0	43	59	11.80
Massie	3	6	0	43	69	11.50
Spofforth	4	6	2	14	31	7.75
Horan	4	7	0	10	49	7.00
Palmer	4	6	2	7	20	5.00
Garrett	3	5	0	10	16	3.20

AUSTRALIA BOWLING

	balls	maidens	runs	wickets	average
Horan	154	16	63	5	12.60
Bannerman	44	2	17	1	17.00
Boyle	252	25	87	5	17.40
Midwinter	278	37	71	4	17.75
Giffen	324	23	164	8	20.50
Palmer	981	113	397	19	20.89
Spofforth	977	93	397	18	22.05
Garrett	412	34	156	3	52.00
Evans	44	3	15	0	
McDonnell	24	0	16	0	

Australia scored 1378 runs for 67 wickets at 20.56

FIRST-CLASS AVERAGES 1882/83
ENGLISH BATTING

	M	I	NO	HS	R	Av
Steel	7	11	1	135*	417	41.70
Leslie	7	11	1	144	310	31.00
Read	7	11	0	75	291	26.45
Bates	7	11	1	55	261	26.10
Barlow	7	11	1	80	248	24.80
Studd C	7	11	0	56	253	23.00
Tylecote	7	11	0	66	209	19.00
Vernon	4	6	1	24	60	12.00
Bligh	5	9	1	19	64	8.00
Studd G	7	11	1	9	40	4.00
Morley	5	7	3	3	9	2.25

ENGLISH BOWLING

	balls	maidens	runs	wickets	average
Leslie	172	18	61	4	15.25
Steel	1128	123	402	25	16.08
Bates	1008	123	346	21	16.47
Read	212	18	92	5	18.40
Barlow	1504	203	437	23	19.00
StuddC	778	118	174	9	19.33
Morley	740	95	190	8	23.75
Barnes	799	75	306	12	25.50

ALL MATCHES

	M	I	NO	HS	R	Av
Steel	17	22	4	135*	551	30.11
Read	17	22	1	84	569	27.20
Leslie	16	21	2	144	484	25.90
Studd C	16	20	0	99	480	24.00
Tylecote	17	21	2	66	438	23.10
Bates	17	22	2	55	422	21.20
Barlow	17	22	1	80	415	19.16
Vernon	14	16	3	41	226	17.50
Studd G	15	19	2	43	230	13.90
Bligh	11	16	1	45	200	13.50
Barnes	17	21	2	32	251	13.40
Morley	9	11	4	3	14	2.00

	balls	maidens	runs	wickets	average
Steel	3200	390	999	152	6.87
Studd C	1786	235	467	60	7.47
Morley	1292	185	324	36	9.00
Bates	2269	299	640	63	10.10
Barnes	1459	155	473	44	10.33
Read	390	36	155	10	15.50
Leslie	192	20	67	4	16.75
Barlow	2181	312	605	36	16.29

Ivo Bligh Career Summary
Season by Season

Season	M	I	NO	HS	R	Ave	100	50	Ct
1877	2	3	0	15	20	6.66	–	–	–
1878	17	25	2	60	375	16.30	–	1	12
1879	21	35	3	113*	614	19.18	1	1	16
1880	21	38	5	105	1013	30.69	1	8	23
1881	11	21	0	78	441	21.00	–	2	21
1882/83	5	9	1	19	64	8.00	–	–	7
1883	7	12	0	42	206	17.16	–	–	2
Total	**84**	**143**	**11**	**113***	**2733**	**20.70**	**2**	**12**	**81**

Appendix D

ENGLAND–AUSTRALIA TEST RESULTS SUMMARY.

Season	England	Australia	Tests	E	A	D	Ashes
1876/77	James Lillywhite	DW Gregory	2	1	1	0	
1878/79	Lord Harris	DW Gregory	1	0	1	0	
1880	Lord Harris	WL Murdoch	1	1	0	0	
1881/82	A Shaw	WL Murdoch	4	0	2	2	
1882	AN Hornby	WL Murdoch	1	0	1	0	Won by Australia
1882/83	Hon. Ivo Bligh	WL Murdoch	4	2	2	0	Won by England
1884	Lord Harris	WL Murdoch	3	1	0	2	England
1884/85	A Shrewsbury	TP Horan	5	3	2	0	England
1886	AG Steel	HJH Scott	3	3	0	0	England
1886/87	A Shrewsbury	P McDonnell	2	2	0	0	England
1887/88	WW Read	P McDonnell	1	1	0	0	England
1888	WG Grace	P McDonnell	3	2	1	0	England
1890	WG Grace	WL Murdoch	2	2	0	0	England
1891/92	WG Grace	J Blackham	3	1	2	0	Australia
1893	WG Grace	J Blackham	3	1	0	2	England
1894/95	AE Stoddart	G Giffen	5	3	2	0	England
1896	WG Grace	GHS Trott	3	2	1	0	England
1897/98	AE Stoddart	GHS Trott	5	1	4	0	Australia
1899	AC MacLaren	J Darllng	5	0	1	4	Australia
1901/02	AC MacLaren	J Darling	5	1	4	0	Australia
1902	AC MacLaren	J Darling	5	1	2	2	Australia
1903/04	PF Warner	MA Noble	5	3	2	0	England
1905	Hon. FS Jackson	J Darling	5	2	0	3	England
1907/08	AO Jones	MA Noble	5	1	4	0	Australia
1909	AC MacLaren	MA Noble	5	1	2	2	Australia
1911/12	JWHT Douglas	C Hill	5	4	1	0	England
1912	CB Fry	SE Gregory	3	1	0	2	Not at stake
1920/21	JWHT Douglas	WW Armstrong	5	0	5	0	Australia
1921	Hon. LH Tennyson	WW Armstrong	5	0	3	2	Australia
1924/25	AER Gilligan	HL Collins	5	1	4	0	Australia
1926	AW Carr	HL Collins	5	1	0	4	England
1928/29	APF Chapman	J Ryder	5	4	1	0	England
1930	APF Chapman	WM Woodfull	5	1	2	2	Australia

1932/33	DR Jardine	WM Woodfull	5	4	1	0	England
1934	RES Wyatt	WM Woodfull	5	1	2	2	Australia
1936/37	GOB Allen	DG Bradman	5	2	3	0	Australia
1938	WR Hammond	DG Bradman	4	1	1	2	Australia
1946/47	WR Hammond	DG Bradman	5	0	3	2	Australia
1948	NWD Yardley	DG Bradman	5	0	4	1	Australia
1950/51	FR Brown	AL Hassett	5	1	4	0	Australia
1953	L Hutton	AL Hassett	5	1	0	4	England
1954/55	L Hutton	IW Johnson	5	3	1	1	England
1956	PBH May	IW Johnson	5	2	1	2	England
1958/59	PBH May	R Benaud	5	0	4	1	Australia
1961	PBH May	R Benaud	5	1	2	2	Australia
1962/63	ER Dexter	R Benaud	5	1	1	3	Australia
1964	ER Dexter	RB Simpson	5	0	1	4	Australia
1965/66	MJK Smith	RB Simpson	5	1	1	3	Australia
1968	MC Cowdrey	WM Lawry	5	1	1	3	Australia
1970/71	R Illingworth	WM Lawry	6	2	0	4	England
1972	R Illingworth	IM Chappell	5	2	2	1	England
1974/75	MH Denness	IM Chappell	6	1	4	1	Australia
1975	AW Greig	IM Chappell	4	0	1	3	Australia
1976/77	AW Greig	GS Chappell	1	0	1	0	Not at stake
1977	JM Brearley	GS Chappell	5	3	0	2	England
1978/79	JM Brearley	GN Yallop	6	5	1	0	England
1979/80	JM Brearley	GS Chappell	3	0	3	0	Not at stake
1980	IT Botham	GS Chappell	1	0	0	1	Not at stake
1981	JM Brearley	KJ Hughes	6	3	1	2	England
1982/83	RGD Willis	GS Chappell	5	1	2	2	Australia
1985	DI Gower	AR Border	6	3	1	2	England
1986/87	MW Gatting	AR Border	5	2	1	2	England
1987/88	MW Gatting	AR Border	1	0	0	1	Not at stake
1989	DI Gower	AR Border	6	0	4	2	Australia
1990/91	GA Gooch	AR Border	5	0	3	2	Australia
1993	GA Gooch	AR Border	6	1	4	1	Australia
1994/95	MA Atherton	MA Taylor	5	1	3	1	Australia
1997	MA Atherton	MA Taylor	6	2	3	1	Australia
1998/99	AJ Stewart	MA Taylor	5	1	3	1	Australia
2001	N Hussain	SR Waugh	5	1	4	0	Australia
2002/03	N Hussain	SR Waugh	5	1	4	0	Australia
2005	M Vaughan	RT Ponting	5	2	1	2	England

Appendix E

THE CHRISTIE'S AUCTION

Catalogue of Important Pictures by Old Masters from Cobham Hall to be sold by Messrs Christie, Manson and Woods May 1st 1925.

1. The Parable of the Loaves and Fishes.
2. Portrait of Sir Philip Sydney.
3. Fruit and other Objects on a Table by Theodoer Aendaenck.
4. Portrait of John Gay, the Poet and Dramatist, by William Aikman.
5. Apollo expelled by the Gods and Goddesses on Mount Olympus by Francesco Albano.
6. Portrait of William Petyt, Esq, by Peter Van Bleek.
7. Portrait of William Shakespeare by William Burbage.
8. The Piazza of St Mark's, Venice by Canaletto.
9. The Church of Santa Maria della Salute, Venice by Canaletto.
10. View of Lucca by Canaletto.
11. The Toilet of Venus by Annibale Carracci.
12. Portrait of Anne, Fourth Wife of Philip ll of Spain, by Coello
13. La Singalla by Correggio.
14. Portrait of Margarita of Austria by Juan Pantoja de la Cruz.
15. Portrait of Thomas Betterton, the Actor and Dramatist, by Michael Dahl.
16. Portrait of a Gentleman by William Dobson.
17. The Archangel Gabriel – Florentine School.
18. Portrait of Miss Theodosia Magill, granddaughter of First Earl of Darnley, by Gainsborough.
19. Portrait of Mrs William Monck, sister to First Earl of Darnley, by Gainsborough.

20. Portraits of Lord John and Lord Bernard Stuart, after Vandyck, by Gainsborough.
21. Portrait of Lord Bernard Stuart, after Vandyck, by Gainsborough.
22. Portrait of Frances Howard, Duchess of Richmond and Lenox, by Marc Gheeraedts.
23. Portrait of a Lady of the Lenox family by Marc Gheeraedts.
24. Portrait of a boy by Marc Gheerhaedts.
25. Portrait of Hieronimus Benivieni by Ridolfo Ghirlandajo.
26. Caesar enthroned receives the Head of Pompey by Giorgione.
27. Portrait of John Locke, the Philosopher by John Greenhill.
28. Portrait of the Artist by Guercino.
29. Portrait of an Artist by Guido Cagnacci.
30. Portrait of a Gentleman by Gerard Honthorst.
31. Portrait of John, Fourth Earl of Darnley by John Hoppner.
32. Portrait of Lady Elizabeth Bligh by John Hoppner.
33. Donatus, Lord O'Brien and Mary, Countess of Kildare when young by Jacob Huysman.
34. Portrait of King James I by Jamesone.
35. Portrait of Jonathan Swift by Charles Jervas.
36. Portrait of a Gentleman by Cornelis Jonson.
37. Portrait of George Villiers, First Duke of Buckingham, by Cornelis Jonson.
38. The Artist and his Wife by Jacob Jordaens.
39. Pomona by Jacob Jordaens.
40. Still Life by Nicolas de Largilliere.
41. Portrait of Charles Stuart, Sixth Duke of Richmond and Lenox, by Sir Peter Lely.
42. Portrait of Dorothy Sydney, Lady Sunderland, by Sir Peter Lely.
43. Portrait of Prince Rupert, by Sir Peter Lely.
44. Portrait of Philip Sidney, Third Earl of Leicester, by Sir Peter Lely.
45. Portrait of a young Nobleman, by Sir Peter Lely.
46. Portrait of Dame Mary Carre, by Sir Peter Lely.
47. Portrait of Sir William Myddleton.

48. Portrait of a youth by Marescalco.
49. A Man in the Attitude of Prayer by Hans Memling.
50. Portrait of Mary Tudor by Sir Antonio Mor.
51. A Man with a Bow and Arrow by Sir Antonio Mor.
52. The Sisters by Paulus Moreelse.
53. A Hilly Landscape by Moucheron.
54. Portrait of Charles I by Daniel Mytens.
55. Interior of a Cathedral by Pieter Neefs.
56. Portrait of Mary Queen of Scots by P. Oudry.
57. Portrait of Francois, Duc D'Alencon, by Pourbus.
58. The Battle between Lapithoe and Centaurs at the Marriage of Pirithous by Poussin.
59. The Preservation of Pyrrhus by Poussin.
60. A Nymph with Satyr and Cupids by Poussin.
61. Bacchus, Ariadne and Cupid by Poussin.
62. Two men holding a Calf by Poussin.
63. The miraculous draught of fishes by Raphael.
64. Portrait of General the Hon. Edward Bligh by Reynolds.
65. Portrait of John, Third Earl of Darnley, by Reynolds.
66. The Calling of Samuel by Reynolds.
67. Portrait of Mrs Gore, sister to First Earl of Darnley, by Reynolds.
68. Portrait of Alexander Pope by Jonathan Richardson.
69. Portrait of Henry St. John, Viscount Bolingbroke, by Jonathan Richardson.
70. Portrait of the Artist by Jonathan Richardson.
71. Atilius Regulus, by Salvator Rosa.
72. Portrait of a Warrior by Salvator Rosa.
73. Jason and the Dragon by Salvator Rosa.
74. Head of an old woman by Rubens.
75. The Flagellation of Christ by Andrea Schiavone.
76. A stag hunt by Snyders.
77. The fable of the hare and the tortoise by Snyders.
78. The interior of a tavern by David Teniers.
79. Venus and Adonis by Titian.
80. Salvator Mundi by Titian.

81. Venus and Cupid holding a mirror by Titian.
82. Titian and Aretino by Titian.
83. Danae by Titian.
84. A wreck on a rocky coast by Willem van de Velde.
85. Portrait of George Stuart, Lord D'Aubigny, by Vandyke.
86. Portrait of James Stuart, Fourth Duke of Lenox and Richmond, by Vandyke.
87. The Madonna and Child with St Elizabeth, by Vandyke.
88. Portrait of Inigo Jones, by Vandyke.
89. Portrait of Lord John Stuart by Vandyke.
90. Christ healing the sick by Benjamin West.
91. Christ expelling the Money Changers by Benjamin West.
92. Portrait of Mary of Modena, wife of James II, by Willem Wissing.

Index